# Last Chance
### The final week of Jesus' life

*by*
James Taylor

with detailed lesson plans for use
in Lenten Bible study groups

**Other books by Jim Taylor**

published by Wood Lake Books
*An Everyday God*
*Two Worlds in One*
*The Canadian Religous Travel Guide*

published by The United Church of Canada
*Life-long Living*

## Canadian Cataloguing in Publication Data

Taylor, James, 1936-
  Last Chance

  ISBN 0-919599-71-0

  1. Jesus Christ - Biography - Passion Week - Meditations. 2. Holy Week - Meditations. I. Title
  BT414.T39 1989   232.9'6   C89-091064-2

All photographs by the author, unless otherwise credited

**Copyright © 1989 James Taylor**
All rights reserved. No part of this publication may be reproduced, stored in a retrieval system, or transmitted in any form or by any means, electronic, mechanical, photocopying, recording, or otherwise, without the prior written permission of the author.

Published by:
Wood Lake Books Inc.,
Box 700, Winfield, BC  V0H 2C0

Printed in Canada by:
Friesen Printers
Altona, MB  R0G 0B0

# Contents

|  |  |  |
|---|---|---|
|  | Preface and dedication | 5 |
| Day 1 | **Ash Wednesday** | 9 |
| Days 2–4 | Daily readings | 16 |
| Day 5 | **First Sunday of Lent** | 21 |
| Days 6–11 | Daily readings | 28 |
|  | Group study, Session One | 36 |
| Day 12 | **Second Sunday of Lent** | 39 |
| Days 13–18 | Daily readings | 46 |
|  | Group study, Session Two | 57 |
| Day 19 | **Third Sunday of Lent** | 59 |
| Days 20–25 | Daily readings | 65 |
|  | Group study, Session Three | 76 |
| Day 26 | **Third Sunday of Lent** | 79 |
| Days 27–32 | Daily readings | 87 |
|  | Group study, Session Four | 95 |
| Day 33 | **Fourth Sunday of Lent** | 97 |
| Days 34–39 | Daily readings | 104 |
|  | Group study, Session Five | 114 |
| Day 40 | **Palm Sunday** | 117 |
| Days 41–44 | Daily readings | 122 |
| Day 45 | **Good Friday** | 129 |
| Day 46 | Daily reading | 134 |
|  | Group study, Session Six | 136 |
| Day 47 | **Easter Sunday** | 139 |

# Preface

This book originated when the ministerial association at Stayner, a small community on Georgian Bay in Ontario, invited me to speak at a series of services during Holy Week 1988.

Because it was Holy Week, I decided to focus, each day, on the events that people would have witnessed had they been in Jerusalem themselves on one of the final days in Jesus' life. I had a suspicion—at that time still vague and ill-formed—that we cheat ourselves of much of the story by knowing how it ends.

My vague and ill-formed suspicion took clearer shape when I listened to the prayers offered by the various ministers who led in worship with me. With one exception, the prayers prepared for those services focussed exclusively on the sacrifice of Jesus on the cross. It felt almost as if nothing that led to the cross mattered, as if the events of that last week in Jerusalem had been blotted out, erased from memory and significance.

Knowing about the cross is a bit like reading the final chapter of a whodunit mystery before you read the rest of the plot. Knowing the ending radically changes your involvement in the story itself. In the Bible, the stark horror of the cross and the overflowing joy of the Resurrection certainly overshadow the preceding events of Holy Week.

But shadows don't fall backwards. The crucifixion could not throw its shadow over other events until it happened. The people who lived through that week didn't know how it would end.

So I tried to present the events of that week as

they might have affected the participants. I treated each event as an opportunity for Jesus to reinforce what he had already tried to teach them. I looked at each event as a culmination of what had gone before, while trying not to let it be colored by what came after.

To my surprise, the people who stayed after the services to talk seemed to find this a novel, even radical, approach. I found myself wondering why. I discussed it with people I met. They too found the approach stimulating. And so, after some nine months of gestation, this book was born.

**About the book**

In writing this book, I have tried to follow the style of my two previous books, *Two Worlds in One* and *An Everyday God*. That is, I have kept most of the items fairly short, suitable for private reading, with a suggested scripture reading and questions for personal meditation.

But recognizing that many congregations gather groups together for Lenten study, I have made a couple of changes. For each Sunday of Lent, for Ash Wednesday which begins Lent, and for Good Friday, I have included a longer piece. These longer pieces explore the major theme, concentrating on one of the events of Holy Week.

Second, I have provided a series of "lesson plans" that congregations could use, if they choose to use this book as the basis for their Lenten study.

Local leaders may want to adapt the content of this book in creating their own sessions. For those who do not feel confident about developing their own theme presentations, I have recorded the major themes—for Ash Wednesday, Good Friday, and each Sunday— on a cassette audio tape, which can be ordered.

**Two non-apologies**

While the main themes developed in this book are entirely a new creation, readers will find that some of the daily meditations have been borrowed from my previous books, from my newsletter *Currents*, or, occasionally, from columns written for the *Anglican Magazine*. I make no apology for this. Most of these examples, these illustrations, come from my own life and experience. I write them in the first person because I want readers to say to themselves: "That kind of thing has happened to me, too."

Those experiences do not become invalid simply because I have used them before. The story I told my daughter when she was 12, I may tell her again when she's 24. But in that time, she has grown and changed; so have I; so has the significance of the story. If I repeat in this book a story that I have previously published elsewhere, I do so because it best illustrates the point I want to make. To choose some weaker illustration—simply because the best one has already been published—would deliberately weaken the book.

I make no apology, either, for including a number of illustrations related to the death of my son, Stephen. I do this not out of any morbid lingering over past grief, nor out of any desire for sympathy. Stephen died more than five years ago, in 1983, and while we continue to miss him, we have learned to live without him. But in a book that examines the events of a week that culminated in a shattering death, I would be dishonest if I avoided his death, the most shattering incident in my own life.

**Dedication**

Many people deserve thanks:
- Ralph Milton and the staff of Wood Lake Books in

Winfield, B.C., who put up with my idiosyncrasies and occasional irritability with good humor, and continue to make me feel valued;

• the ministerial association at Stayner—especially Maurice Francis, the United Church minister there—who formally invited me to give the sermons that led to this book;

• John Bird, editor of the *Anglican Magazine*, whose deadlines repeatedly force me to search out new insights;

• the little Bible study group that has met for eight years at Parkwoods United Church in Toronto, whose perceptions and struggles help me recognize the wisdom of ordinary readers of scripture;

• and all the readers of *An Everyday God*, of *Two Worlds in One*, and of the *Currents* newsletter, whose letters and comments reassure me that I have something worth saying.

But in a book dealing with the undeserved death of its central character, I can only dedicate this book one way.

To
**Joan and Sharon**
who lived through our Black Friday with me
with love

**Jim Taylor,**
January 1989

**Day 1** *Ash Wednesday*

# One final week

Imagine, for a moment, that you had just one more week to live. What would you try to do in that week?

In one week, you couldn't possibly complete everything you dreamed of doing. There wouldn't be time to travel to Tahiti, to climb Mount Everest, to write a novel, to be elected to high office.... One week is too short a time. The closeness of the end would probably overwhelm you—along with the paralyzing fear that you'd soon be forgotten.

Most of us, I suspect, are less afraid of *dying* than of *disappearing*. We can face death with varying degrees of courage. But the prospect of being forgotten, of vanishing without being missed—that really haunts us. It implies that there was nothing worth remembering about our lives. Whether or not we believe in eternal life, we still want to be remembered.

If you knew you only had one week left, the task of making sure you were remembered would probably dominate your final days. How would you do it? With generous gifts? With kind words? With final thoughts, carefully inscribed in letters to be opened only after your death?

That's precisely the problem that faced Jesus, as he came up to what we now call Holy Week. For three years, his words and actions had infuriated influential people. Time after time, his stories had made community leaders look like fools. He had punctured their pretences, and deflated their pomposity. He exposed their narrow legalism and their hypocrisy; he called them "whitewashed tombs," and cautioned people against their example.

As long as he did his preaching, teaching, and healing in far-off Galilee, the nation's boondocks, they might have tolerated his trouble-making. But now he was coming to Jerusalem for Passover. He would be confronting the social and political leaders of the nation on their own turf.

Those leaders had already indicated that they were not prepared to tolerate him. At least once before, according to John's narrative, Jesus had fled from Judea to keep from being stoned by an angry mob (John 10:22–40). The temple authorities had already plotted to get rid of him (John 11:47–53). They were hardly likely to turn the other cheek when he showed up again.

Yet he had to go to Jerusalem. He was, in his own eyes, a devout Jew. Jesus never had any intentions of starting a new religion; he wanted to reform the faith he belonged to; he wanted to renew his nation's awareness of its special role in the world as God's agents, God's people. And despite the antagonism between him and the religious establishment, he remained a devout Jew.

All male Jews were expected to go to Jerusalem for the Passover. So he went. But he knew he might not come back.

Life was cheap in those days. In our relatively safe world, we can afford lofty principles about the sanctity of individual human life. In Jesus' time, people had no such delusions. Life was short anyway, with an average life expectancy of 35 to 40 years. Life was even shorter for those who risked the ire of the ruling authorities. The Roman army occupying the country crushed rebellions with brutal efficiency; the various Herods had a reputation for ruthlessness. Those who escaped these forces fell prey to disease, to accident, to zealots—the "freedom-fighters" of that time—or simply to poverty and deprivation.

Jesus knew that if he caused trouble, he could easily be snuffed out, with no inquest or inquiry, no questions asked. One more death, more or less, would make little difference to anyone but the victim's close friends and family.

Yet in Jerusalem, of all places, he could not keep quiet. He could not simply perform his Jewish religious rituals and slip quietly away. Not without compromising his own principles. Not without betraying the God who was as close as a beloved parent—one whom Jesus spoke of, not as Lord or Master, but as *Abba*—Daddy.

Jesus must have known he had very little time left. And the question pf being remembered must have haunted him, too, as he led the way towards Jerusalem with his reluctant band of followers trailing behind, arguing about who deserved the highest honors. Would they remember him when he was gone? And *how* would they remember him?

Jesus knew that he had been popular. People had crowded around to hear his parables, or to see him heal a cripple or a leper, a man blind from birth or a girl demented by an evil spirit. But crowds had also flocked to hear John the Baptist. And when John was first imprisoned, then beheaded, there had been no popular uprising, no hue and cry, no demands for an investigation to probe the judicial system.

Jesus himself had seen huge crowds flock to him and then fade away at the first hint of political opposition. When he was gone, would they simply turn to the next popular speaker, the next star on the Messiah circuit?

Had the crowds simply seen him as entertainment?

How could he make sure that his message didn't die with him?

The prospect of death, as Samuel Johnson would

observe many centuries later, wonderfully concentrates the mind. I'm convinced that in that last week of his life, Jesus stopped *telling* people his message, and started *showing* them. Every culture contains a saying like the English maxim, "Actions speak louder than words." In that last week, Jesus started acting out his parables.

In one sense, it certainly worked. The first three gospels each devote about a third of their contents to that final week; John's gospel gives it more attention than all the rest of Jesus' ministry. Clearly, the events impressed themselves on the disciples' memory.

It's also the only explanation that I can see for some utterly uncharacteristic actions. There is no indication anywhere else in the gospels that Jesus resorted to violence. Yet two times in that last week, he seems to have chosen violent physical action. In one of those times, he stormed through part of the temple, scattering traders and money changers like chickens before a runaway tractor. In the other, he killed a fig tree.

An innocent fig tree!

Apparently Jesus wanted a fig to eat. But he couldn't, because the fig tree had only leaves on it. So he cursed the tree. Later, as the group passed the tree again, the disciples noted that the tree had withered and died (Mark 11:12–14, 20–25; Matthew 21:18–22).

But the fault, if any, lay with Jesus, not the tree. The Passover is the wrong season for figs. Figs would not form—let alone ripen—for several months yet. *No* fig tree would have had ripe figs on it. And Jesus knew very well that he couldn't expect ripe figs at that time of year. He even used the fig trees ripening as an illustration of predictability, in the parable which started, "Learn a lesson from the fig-tree..." (Matthew 24:32–33; Mark 13:28–29; Luke 21:29–31).

If Jesus destroyed that tree simply because it could

not satisfy an irrational whim, his action was capricious, unjustified, and even malicious.

People today react with rage when they read newspaper stories about pet owners who find their pets inconvenient, and who throw kittens out of cars at high speed or leave puppies in a carton to be incinerated. If Jesus really killed that tree simply because it had denied him fruit, he took out his personal pique on an innocent victim that could just as easily have been a puppy.

His action, in fact, was no more justified than his own crucifixion.

Why then would he do it? Only because he didn't intend his action to be taken literally. It was a symbolic action. Instead of *telling* a parable, he *acted* one.

We need to remember that Jesus was not just a teacher, in the modern sense of the word, who instructed people in an academic discipline. He was a story-teller, a poet, a spinner of words and tales. He knew that all good stories build upon earlier stories. Even if we don't recognize the connections, a movie like "Raiders of the Lost Ark" capitalizes on the story of St. George and the Dragon. The protagonist of any credible novel contains a bit of Hamlet, the villain contains a bit of Hansel and Gretel's witch.

So Jesus constantly alluded to other stories in his parables. Jesus could describe Israel as a vineyard, because the prophet Isaiah had done the same years before (Isaiah 5:1-7). When Jesus spoke of scattering seeds, his hearers heard "seeds" as both a literal description and as God's promise about the descendants of Abraham. When Jesus called himself a shepherd, he triggered associations to countless references to God as shepherd in the Hebrew scriptures—among them what we call the 23rd Psalm.

Jeremiah—a prophet whom Jesus knew as well as most of us know fairy tales—had once spun his own parable around some figs.

"Jeremiah, what do you see?" God had asked Jeremiah.

"Some figs," Jeremiah replied. "Some are good, and some are rotten, fit only to be thrown out."

"So are the people of Israel," God explained. "Some of Israel is still as good as those good figs, and some has rotted. I will take care of the good, but I will treat the bad parts of Israel like those rotten figs that are too bad to eat" (paraphrased from Jeremiah 24:1–10).

In that context, a fig tree that fails to produce fruit takes on a symbolic value. It stands for Israel, which had been nurtured by God for centuries, and yet failed to produce the fruit God wanted. Jesus specifically makes that connection in a spoken parable in Luke's gospel (Luke 13:6–9). There, Jesus suggested, the owner was willing to give a fruitless tree one more chance. If, with some care and nurturing, it produced good fruit, it could live. If not, it would be destroyed.

Just like the fig tree that Jesus destroyed.

Jesus gave much the same message in a parable repeated in all of the first three gospels, the parable of the tenants in the vineyard (Matthew 21:33–43; Mark 12:1–9; Luke 20:9–16). The tenants began to think they owned the farm they rented. When the owner sent servants to reclaim his property, the tenants beat them and threw them out. When the owner sent his heir, the tenants killed him. "What do you suppose the owner will do with those servants?" Jesus asked. "Why, he'll come and kick them out, and turn the vineyard over to others."

That was the message of the withered fig tree, too. But it was *acted*, not *told*.

If you find that concept hard to grasp, it's because

we have traditionally paid much more attention to Jesus' words than his actions. We even have "Red-Letter Bibles," which emphasize Jesus' words with red ink. That practice reduces everything else to grey background. For most of us, in fact, the story of Jesus' life is little more than a way of linking together his teachings.

So it seems strange to look at Jesus' actions instead of his words. Yet I think it's an important principle that helps us understand that last week of his life much better—or at the very least, that gives us a fresh look at a story that has become almost too familiar.

In that one week, Jesus had his last chance to get his point across, his last chance to etch his message permanently into memory.

If we concentrate only on the words he used, we have to read the stories of that last week as a series of unconnected incidents. By the end, Jesus becomes little more than a helpless pawn of powerful forces, tossed from trial to trial, beaten and broken, and finally defeated by death.

But if we read that last week as a series of deliberately enacted parables, we will get quite a different picture.

### Reading: Mark 11:12–14, 20–25
### The blasted fig tree

*Have you ever taken flowers home, after a quarrel?*
*Or silently undertaken a difficult task,*
*to spare someone you love doing it?*
*Why did you act out your emotions,*
*instead of just using words?*

**Day 2** *Thursday*

Everything we do says something about us.

Teenagers wear T-shirts emblazoned with pictures of their favorite rock stars, to proclaim their loyalties—or their revolt against their parents' values, perhaps—without resorting to words.

A woman wearing a double-breasted suit and carrying a boxy brown leather briefcase proclaims by her clothing that she works in a man's world—and she's going to be just as good as any man.

Every time any of us gets dressed in the morning, we act out the kind of people we expect to be that day.

Car manufacturers have long known that we act out our fantasies in the cars we choose. I suspect that one's choice of car reveals as much as any psychoanalyst's couch. Sadists drive those ugly four-wheel-drive trucks perched high atop huge knobbly tires. Aggressive people choose Corvettes and Cobra replicas—merely

*My first British sports cars was a Triumph—and also a disaster...*

sitting in them makes a milquetoast feel macho. People with delusions of grandeur drive Audis; those who would love to have delusions of grandeur someday drive BMWs; those who no longer need delusions drive Mercedes. People with split personalities, presumably, drive turbo-diesels.

Masochists, of course, drive British sports cars. I should know. I've owned two of them—which probably also suggests I'm a slow learner.

The things we do reveal as least as much about us as the things we say.

### Reading: Matthew 7:21–23
### Self-deception

*What clothes did you choose to wear today?*
*What impression did you expect to convey?*

*... So is the second British sports car. But when I drive it with the top down, people seem to envy me...*

**Day 3**                                         *Friday*

When our son Stephen died, many people expressed sympathy. They called us on the telephone. They came to visit. They wrote cards and notes.

But the most powerful expressions of sympathy didn't use words at all.

Mary McCowan came up our driveway. She didn't say a word. Perhaps she didn't trust herself to speak. But she thrust a casserole covered in aluminum foil, still hot from her oven, into my hands. Then she hurried back to her car.

Penny Battle rang the doorbell, and stood there with tears streaming down her face. When Joan opened the door, Penny opened her arms.

Bob and Marion Little simply said, "We're coming over." Then they drove 100 kilometres, to stay with us for six hours, helping us cope with our phone calls, our visitors, our grief.

Words matter. But sometimes our actions speak even louder.

### Reading: John 11:33–35
### Jesus wept

*Remember a time of grief.*
*Remember the people who came without flowery words,*
*just to be there with you.*
*Might they have been acting out their beliefs?*

**Day 4**  *Saturday*

Our scientific age places great value on words. But we have trouble dealing with symbolism.

Symbolic truths aren't precise, like mathematics. They're subjective, not objective; they point to something instead of defining it. They relate to our experience, not our intellect.

Edythe Stockton told me about a friend, years ago, who spent a whole summer working as a sales clerk in a store. She hated the job, but needed the money. Every day, she crammed her feet into a pair of tight red shoes, because she was supposed to "look good" on the job.

At the end of August, she left the store for the last time. She could have just gone home. But her freedom demanded something more.

So she and Edythe walked out to the edge of town, made a small pile of leaves and sticks, put the red shoes on top, and lit the pile.

For all practical purposes, burning those shoes was a meaningless act. It accomplished nothing. In a town struggling for economic survivial, it was wasteful, even extravagant.

But as a symbol, burning those shoes was a declaration of freedom far more powerful than hiding them in a closet or throwing them in the garbage.

To this day, Edythe remembers standing with her friend, watching the despised months dissolve into the prairie sky in a thin column of smoke....

### Reading: Leviticus 1:1–3, 8–9
### Burnt offerings

*Think back to your formative years.*
*What kind of memories stick in your mind?*
*Are those memories mainly of something someone said?*
*Or of something someone did?*

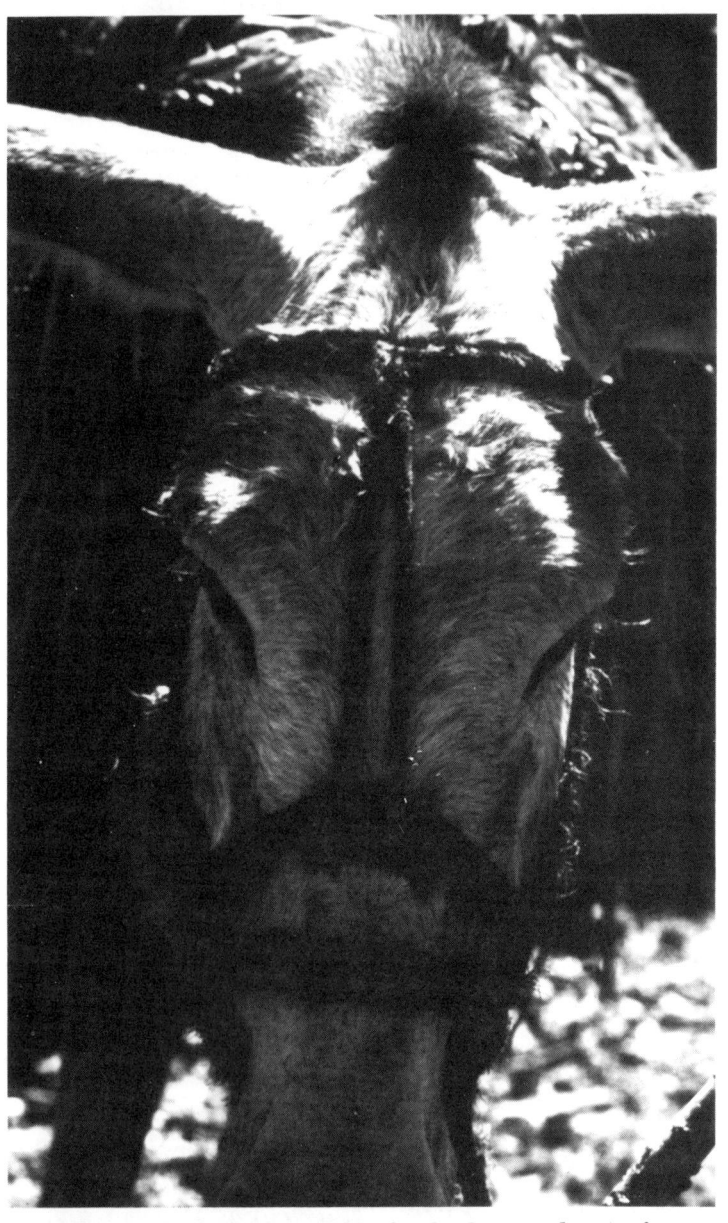

*Almost anywhere in the world, the donkey is a beast of burden, a symbol of humility...*

**Day 5**                                *First Sunday of Lent*

# *Riding on a donkey*

Perhaps the first act, in what we call Passion Week or Holy Week, most clearly indicated Jesus' intentions.

In entering Jerusalem, he acted out a message. Like the enacted parable of the figs, it depended on a scriptural allusion. But for those who knew Hebrew scriptures and traditions, the message would be unmistakable.

Some five centuries earlier, the prophet Zechariah had written about the coming of the promised Messiah. "Rejoice," said Zechariah, "for your king comes to you... riding on a donkey..." (Zechariah 9:9).

Zechariah's choice of animal was significant, because it contradicted popular assumptions about the nature of a Messiah.

Then as now, people thought in power terms. They suffered from what I sometimes call the "Superman Syndrome." That is, they expect the Messiah, the Savior, to act like a fairy godmother and to make things right by waving a magic wand. "Zzzappp!"—everything's fixed! Superman differs from fairy godmothers only in that he settles problems with his fists instead of with a magic wand, and the sound effects change from "Zap" to "Ka-***POW!***"

Fairy godmothers and Superman belong in children's stories and comic books. But the syndrome, the pattern of thinking, continues to afflict adults. Adults wouldn't dream of asking a boss to "kiss it better," or of waiting for a fairy godmother to clean up the yard. But adults buy lottery tickets, hoping that unearned wealth can solve their family problems. Or they elect a handsome but vacuous politician, to restore national prosperity. Or, for that matter, they beg a charismatic television evangelist to cure cancer.

The Superman Syndrome, basically, expects some external authority to do for us what we cannot or will not do for ourselves.

In Jesus' time, people expected their promised Savior to run the hated Roman army out of their territory, and restore Israel to the glory it had known, briefly, under David and Solomon.

Even their choice of era reflects their "Superman Syndrome." Significantly, they didn't think of restoring Israel to its stature under, say, Joshua, when they were a small band of interlopers trying to gain a foothold in a foreign land. Nor to the time of the Exile, even though many Jews had risen to positions of authority within the conquering empire. Nor to their homeless wandering in the wilderness, under Moses. Only the glory of David and Solomon—when they themselves were the "Supermen" of the region—would do.

So they hoped for a new David who could drive out the enemy, demolish opposing religions, and dominate the surrounding territory. Such a leader would return to his capital city in triumphal procession, laden with plunder. He would bring home so much wealth that people could afford to throw their finest clothing on the streets to be trampled beneath the hooves of horses and crushed beneath the wheels of great chariots. Such a leader would *have* to ride on a mighty warhorse.

But Zechariah put the Messiah, the long-promised Savior of Israel, on a donkey. Not a war-horse.

Almost anywhere in the world, the donkey is a symbol of humility. They're beasts of burden. Women ride donkeys. Men, characteristically, feel humiliated on a donkey; if they can't have a horse, or at the least a mule, they'd rather walk. Not by chance do our Christmas cards show *Mary* riding a donkey en route to Bethlehem (although the Bible itself says nothing at all about their means of travel). In the Middle East, in India, in Africa, pregnancy rarely wins special treatment for women; the macho mentality, not necessarily compassion for his partner, would have kept Joseph's feet on the ground.

(New Testament scholar William Barclay argues that among the Hebrews a donkey was not a despised beast but a noble one, because it was used by kings. "When a king went to war, he rode on a horse, when he came in peace he rode on an ass," Barclay says in several commentaries. I suggest that the tradition proves exactly the opposite—any king who arrived on a such a pathetic creature *must* be coming in peace.)

In placing the Messiah on a donkey, Zechariah dramatized a concept that had been around since at least Isaiah's time. Whoever wrote chapters 40–55 of Isaiah, and especially the famous "Suffering Servant" chapters, recognized a profound truth—salvation would never come through power. Superman may bring fast fast relief, like some headache remedies, but it can never be more than temporary relief. When Superman leaves, the incompetent victims are back on their own again. In the same way, Isaiah and Zechariah recognized that no political or military triumph over neighboring nations could last long. Unless the Messiah immediately terminated history (in which case there isn't much point in achieving glory and affluence), or ruled forever (which would result in inflexible and rigid patterns of life, eliminating any hope of change, growth, or progress).

Of course, Zechariah was only a minor prophet. I suspect that human nature hasn't changed very much over the centuries. Most people learn only enough about their religion to get by. So possibly only a limited number of Jews would know about Zechariah and his prophecy that the promised Messiah would come riding, not on a war-horse, but on a donkey.

But there doesn't seem any doubt that Jesus knew Zechariah's prophecy. Certainly, he knew of Isaiah's vision of God's way of working with the world. Perhaps more than anyone else, Isaiah shaped Jesus' ministry. Jesus had tried to get those ideas across to his disciples. He had explained how his kind of leadership meant giving up pretensions of glory. It meant losing any ambitions for your own life, becoming a servant, loving your enemies instead of destroying them.

He even snarled at his disciples when they missed the point. He had asked, "Who do you say that I am?"

Peter, in a great flash of insight, blurted out, "You are the Messiah."

Heartened by this affirmation, Jesus described what it meant to be a Messiah—that he would be betrayed, deserted, put to death. But Peter showed that he still didn't understand. He took Jesus by the arm and tried to correct him: "You've got it all wrong," he told Jesus, in effect. "That's not how Messiahs do things!"

Jesus turned on him, using words as harsh as he used on anyone: "Get away from me, you devil!" Then, perhaps to explain the reason for his anger, Jesus added, "You think the way everyone else thinks, not the way God thinks" (Matthew 16:13–23; Mark 8:27–33; Luke 9:18–22).

In that final week, his last chance to get his message across, Jesus must have despaired of more words. So he decided to act out his message in a way that his followers could neither mistake nor forget. He chose to ride a donkey when he entered Jerusalem.

The gospels tell us, beyond any question, that this was a deliberate choice. Jesus didn't just happen to see a donkey, and decide, "My feet hurt; I think I'll ride for a while." Rather, he knew he wanted a donkey; he knew where he could get one; and he sent his disciples out to bring it to him (Matthew 21:1–9; Mark 11:1–10; Luke 19:28–38; John 12:12–16).

It was deliberate.

And unique. The Bible contains no other record of him riding on an animal of any kind. He walked. He went aboard boats. But apparently he didn't ride. That in itself would make this a memorable event.

Later that week, perhaps in Bethany at the home of his old friends Mary, Martha, and Lazarus, he may have explained to his disciples his reasons for choosing the donkey, just as he obviously explained some parables in private. Or possibly some biblically-literate person put two and two together, after the fact, and realized the significance of Jesus' action.

However that understanding came, all the gospel writers grasped it. So did Paul. Writing to the Philippians, he quotes what may have been a hymn or a creed of the early church:

*Being of the very nature of God,*
*he humbled himself...* (Philippians 2:6,7)

That idea of humility, of being willing to be less than one could be, less than one was entitled to be, turns conventional wisdom upside down. One is expected to aspire to greater things, not lesser. We still *prize* upward mobility; we *sympathize* with those who experience downward mobility through aging, retirement, firing, unemployment, divorce, death....

But Jesus consistently set an example of humbling himself. He played with children, treated women as friends, and associated with lepers and tax collectors—

all whom the men of his day treated with contempt. But his two most dramatic demonstrations of humility came during that final week of his life—when he rode a donkey... and rode a cross.

When we read the stories of Palm Sunday, we place too much emphasis on the triumphal entry, not enough on his choice of a mount.

In fact, if Jesus enacted a parable in order to teach us, then his *choice* is the more important element. He had no more control over the mob that shouted "Hosanna!" than he had over the mob that later shouted "Crucify him!" But clearly he and only he decided that he would ride into Jerusalem on a donkey.

In concentrating on the acclaim of the crowd, we distort the message he intended. We glorify popularity and social approval. We subvert the Suffering Servant, making him match our human notions of royalty; we put Jesus on a pedestal.

The procession celebrates pomp and pageantry. It turns his enacted parable into precisely the kind of triumphant military procession that riding on a donkey was supposed to contradict.

I suspect that there may have been a fair amount of mockery in those "Hosanna's" anyway. Mobs are never noted for their empathy with suffering victims. The same kind of people who gather at the midway of a big fair or exhibition today would have gathered by the city gates during a Jewish festival. They were looking for entertainment, and they didn't care much who provided it. And sure enough, here comes a man, riding on a donkey. His friends claim this is the promised Messiah? What a hoot! Let's have some fun with him; let's act as if he were a returning hero....

So they shout "Save us! Save us!" (a literal translation of "Hosanna") to a nobody from Nazareth riding a pathetic beast of burden.

In that context, "Hosanna" has a hollow ring.

But the choice of a donkey doesn't. It still conveys the message that Jesus wanted to convey. It tells us that God's way is peace, not war. It is humility, not power. It is service, not status. It recognizes our common humanity, rather than emphasizing our differences.

In choosing a donkey, Jesus acted out a parable for his disciples. It's time we paid more attention to what he was trying to teach us, too.

### Reading: Matthew 21:1-11
### The entry into Jerusalem

*Has anything that you've done been misunderstood?*
*Were your good intentions taken as malice,*
*or your kindness as meddling?*
*How did you feel when people got the wrong message?*
*How do you think Jesus might feel*
*when we keep getting his message mixed up?*

# Day 6 — Monday

A young couple sat at the next restaurant table, telling friends about trekking in Nepal. I eavesdropped shamelessly.

They talked about the magnificence of Himalayan peaks, about paths that clung to the sides of cliffs as if glued on, about Nepali porters carrying 150-pound loads of charcoal over passes high above the tree line...

Then she talked about getting sick. "I don't know what it was, really," she said. "Malaria, dysentery...? There were no doctors around to diagnose it."

"We had to hike out, before we could get any help," he chimed in.

"I really didn't think I'd make it," she continued. "I just wanted to lie down and go to sleep. All the time, John kept encouraging me. Then even his pep talks didn't work. Finally, he just said, 'Kate! Follow my feet!' I didn't have the strength to lift my head up to look around. All I could see were his boots, squishing

in the mud of the trail, right in front of me. I just kept putting my foot down where his had just been."

"And we made it," he concluded, triumphantly.

We keep trying to reduce Jesus' teaching to a set of principles, or a collection of instructions—something we can argue over and find loopholes in. Yet what he really tells us, over and over, is to take him as a living example, to follow his feet.

### Reading: Luke 5:27–28
### "Follow me"

*Remember, when you were a child, how secure you felt*
*holding your mother's hand while crossing the street?*
*How secure do you feel about life*
*now that you're on your own?*
*Would you like that sense of assurance again?*
*Could you find it, following Jesus?*

Government of India photo

*Riding on a donkey*

**Day 7** *Tuesday*

The Passion Play in the little village of Oberammergau, in the Bavarian mountains, opens on an empty stage.

Then people begin spilling onto the stage. Dozens. Scores. Hundreds. They come out of doorways, alleys, streets, and gates. More people than I've ever seen on a stage before at one time. During crowd scenes, the shops close, the schools send children in rows of buses—the whole village, it seems, crowds onto the stage.

A babble of excited conversation fills the theater. Then it turns into a chant. The chant spreads, until everyone is shouting, "Hosanna! Hosanna!"

Sitting in the audience, I looked around to find Jesus in the crowd. Surely, I thought, he would be easy to recognize. He would stand out from everyone else....

Somehow, I expected him to stand head and shoulders above everyone else—taller, straighter, more authoritative, a larger-than-life figure....

And I couldn't find him.

In the end, I could only tell which person was Jesus by looking for the donkey. Jesus must be the one riding it. Otherwise, he looked like everyone else.

It made me wonder how often I might have missed him in other settings, where I had no donkey to help me.

### Reading: Zechariah 9:9–10
### Riding on a donkey

*Have you ever met someone you know well*
*in an unfamiliar setting?*
*And failed to recognize them?*
*Do you really know them as well as you think you do?*
*Or do you see only your own expectations?*

**Day 8**                                   *Wednesday*

Years ago, during a camp weekend in the Gulf of Georgia, a group gathered for worship under a canopy of trees.

The leader called for silent prayer.

After a while, I realized I could hear two watches ticking. Somebody near me had a watch ticking at exactly the same speed as my own. When the prayer ended, I looked around. Dave Reuss, a friend sitting about four feet away, was also looking around.

"Was that *your* watch?" I whispered.

He nodded. "Wasn't it *fantastic?*" he whispered back.

The incident sticks in my memory, because in the last 20 years I don't think I've heard the sound of my own watch —unless I put it right up to my ear—let alone someone else's watch some distance away. In our technological culture, silence is an endangered species.

Inside the house, if the refrigerator isn't running, the furnace is. In the office, computers whir and typewriters click; fluorescent lights hum and telephones ring; somewhere a radio always prattles mindlessly.

In restaurants and bars, the chatter is thicker than the cigarette smoke.

What is it about crowds and noise that attracts us, I wonder?

And is that why we pay attention to the "Hosanna's" on Palm Sunday, and avoid the sorrowful silence of the man on the donkey?

### Reading: Zechariah 2:10–13
### Silence in the Lord's presence

*Where do you go for holidays and entertainment?*
*Where lots of other people also go?*
*Would you go there if no one else did?*

*Riding on a donkey*

# Day 9　　　　　　　　　　　　　　*Thursday*

Driving to an appointment, I flicked on the car radio. Program host Peter Gzowski was interviewing a jazz musician who had spent a year studying music in Burma and Thailand.

The musician started talking about temple bells. Not the kind of bells we know in our churches, which hang high in steeples to chime out the hours or to call people to worship.

These eastern bells hang *inside* the temple. And they're played like musical instruments. Each bell has its own note. And each one is carefully cast, carefully tuned, to the temple it hangs in.

The musician described one big bell he had seen in a temple. "If you took it outside the temple and struck it," he said, "it would make a dull, flat clang. You couldn't hear it twenty yards away. But when you hit it inside the temple, it can be heard for two or three miles!"

"Why?" Peter wondered.

"Because its vibrations resonate with the natural frequencies of the whole temple," the musician explained. "The building amplifies the sounds of the bell."

Peter commented: "In a sense, you're not playing the bell as much as the temple itself!"

In the North American cult of individualism, we each assume that our value depends on what each of us achieves on our own. We try to act alone. Like a bell taken out into the open air and struck.

And all we seem to produce in our lives is a dull clang.

Perhaps, instead of trying to sing solos, we should try to strike notes in our lives that will resonate through our communities.

If Jesus had tried to do it all by himself, he would

Government of India photo

probably have ended up as little more than a footnote to history. Jesus rang bells for the world only when his community of followers began to resonate to his song.

### Reading: John 17:20–23
### That all may be one

*What do you dream about, in your future?*
*Fame? Fortune? Peace? Harmony?*
*Could your dreams come true, all by yourself?*
*Or must you also inspire others,*
*to resonate with your vision?*

# Day 10 — Friday

Joan makes the best pancakes in the world. I can claim that on the best possible authority—our children's reaction to her pancakes.

But don't ask Joan for the recipe. There isn't one.

Joan just dumps flour into the mixing bowl until the pile looks about right, adds about the right splotch of baking powder, an egg or two, and pours in milk until it makes the right size puddle.

Over the years, we tried to measure all these actions, and to write them down. But when we make pancakes according the the recipe that emerges, they never taste quite the same.

Fortunately, our daughter Sharon is getting pretty good at preparing pancakes too. She doesn't use a recipe either. But she's watched Joan enough, and tried it enough, that she knows how big to make the pile of flour, how deep to make the puddle of milk.

Following Jesus is a bit like Joan's pancakes. We keep expecting to find a recipe that will make it easy. We look for it in the Bible, in Sunday sermons, in books about theology.

But maybe there isn't a recipe. Maybe we just have to learn how by doing it ourselves.

### Reading: Luke 9:1-2
### Sending out

*How did you first learn to ride a bicycle?*
*By doing it, of course.*
*How are you trying to learn to be Christian?*

**Day 11**  *Saturday*

One summer, Joan and I visited Bonaventure Island, off the Gaspé Peninsula.

The whole island is a sanctuary for nesting seabirds. Especially gannets. Thousands of the great white seabirds have built their nests on tiny ledges of the cliffs. Many thousands more cluster along the cliffs.

"The harder a nest is to get at, the safer it is from predators like weasels," explained a park naturalist. "Gannets mate for life, and every year, the pair comes back to exactly the exact spot where they nested when they first matured."

The young gannets probably have no idea of the significance of the decision they're making when they choose their first nesting site. They grab whatever they can, wherever it is. And yet their choice affects their own survival, the survival of their one egg a year, the survival of their genetic strain....

The implications of one apparently insignificant choice—where to build a nest—ripple infinitely into the future.

We can't foresee the implications of our own seemingly minor decisions: whether or not to go to university, what kind of job to take, when to have children, how to rear them.... Yet each decision, once made, can't be altered. For better or for worse, it affects everything that follows.

Our choices are never unimportant.

**Reading: Deuteronomy 30:11–20a**
**Choose life.**

*Some people were born blessed;*
*others have had to struggle every step of the way.*
*Which matters more—what they are now?*
*Or the choices they had to make, to get there?*
*How about your choices?*

## Session One

> **Please note**
> This study program was planned to have six sessions, one during each week following each Sunday in Lent. If you find it impossible to schedule a six-week program, we recommend leaving out Session Three.
>
> If even five sessions is too long, you may choose to leave out another session, or try to combine two sessions. Session 1 and 2 may be the easiest to combine, concentrating on the concept that "actions speak louder than words" and using the cleansing of the Temple mainly as an example of those actions.

### Purpose
This session deals with the subjects of Days 1-11, including the main themes of Ash Wednesday and the 1st Sunday of Lent. All of the readings for this period stress the idea that "actions speak louder than words."

### Preparation
Ensure that all participants have copies of the book. Ideally, they should receive their copies in advance, so that they can read the book daily and come informed.

If they cannot receive books in advance, have enough copies on hand for all registrants. Under no circumstances should they have to wait another week before receiving a book to read.

Set up the room so that people will be able to see each other—and not just the backs of each others' heads! For small groups, the chairs could form a circle; for larger numbers, perhaps a semi-circle with two or three rows.

### Getting started
Open with prayer or singing or both.

Have people introduce themselves by giving their names, any other information they consider significant (such as "I'm so-and-so's grandmother" or "I teach Sunday School"). *Have them also describe, in a few sentences, something they did today that's fairly characteristic of their lives.*

### Getting involved
Brainstorm old sayings. Invite people to call out maxims they heard from their parents or grandparents, and write them onto a blackboard or flipchart. (Examples might be: "A stitch in time saves nine," or "Penny

wise, pound foolish.") If no one calls out, "Actions speak louder than words," "Do as I do, not as I say," or "Experience is the best teacher," add them to the list yourself during the brainstorming process.

The purpose of brainstorming is to get as many people as possible involved. Remember the cardinal rule of brainstorming: No idea is ever rejected or ridiculed! Brainstorming helps to set the pattern for later discussion—it assures people that their thoughts are worth sharing with others, and will not be made fun of.

When you have a sheet or two pretty well covered with old sayings, underline or highlight in some way those that emphasize actions. (All of them may!)

### Starting the thoughts

Point out the wisdom of those sayings which stress vigorous action rather than wimpy words.

Using the concepts in the major pieces for Ash Wednesday and the 1st Sunday of Lent, suggest that looking at Jesus' actions during his last week of life, rather than his words, can give us some startling new perspectives on what he wanted us to learn. You might as well admit that this approach will surprise some people and disturb others. And it may require a deliberate setting aside of people's previous understandings.

For example, they have probably thought of Jesus' entry to Jerusalem as a triumph. The book suggests it may well have been based on mockery, a desire for entertainment, even ridicule. The book further suggests that we should be concentrating not on the crowd, with Jesus as passive participant, but on what Jesus himself did when he chose to ride on a donkey.

Expand as much as you want on the concept of teaching by acting out a message. One of the daily readings may help to ground this principle in real-life experience.

(If you don't feel competent to undertake this presentation of concepts on your own, you may prefer to purchase the cassette tape in which the author reads from the Ash Wednesday and 1st Sunday pieces.)

### Grounding thoughts in scripture

Have everyone find the Old Testament foundation for Jesus' choice of a donkey, Zechariah 9:9–10. Read it aloud in unison.

Then find Jesus' entry to Jerusalem, Matthew 21:1–11. Suggest to the participants that, as they read this passage aloud, they also reflect on how the ideas that have just been presented affect their perceptions of these familiar words. Read the passage together.

### Applying new understandings to life

If the group is small, say ten or fewer, continue discussion as a whole group. If it is larger, divide up into smaller discussion groups. If possible, no group should be smaller than six; eight is about ideal; beyond twelve, some people always get left out.

Assign each group three topics to discuss, to deal with as fully as possible, as time permits. (If you prefer, you may create your own questions for stimulating discussion, based perhaps on some of the questions associated with the daily readings.)

1. *Which are more memorable—actions or words? Why?* Encourage participants to share some of their own memories of words or actions, and to explain why they were so memorable. (Remember that as with brainstorming, this kind of question has no right or wrong answers. It's possible to challenge someone's interpretation of an experience, but not the experience itself.)

2. *If you had only a limited time left to live, what kind of message would you want to get across to someone? To whom? How?* Encourage people to be specific. What would they say? What would they do? As they talk about this, can they see better why Jesus might have chosen to do the things he did?

3. *Why don't you convey that message to that person now, instead of waiting?* This may evoke reactions, that the other person won't listen, isn't ready yet, etc. In that case, is that "other person" like Jesus' disciples? Are any of us ready to hear Jesus' message? If we were, how might it change our lives?

### Putting it together

If you have divided into several groups for discussion, gather together again.

Invite participants to volunteer insights they may have gained during the discussion. (Sometimes one person will want to draw attention to an insight or discovery someone else seemed to have—that's quite acceptable.)

Avoid, if possible, a reporting by a leader of what groups discussed.

### Closing

End with prayer, music if appropriate, and a blessing or benediction.

**Day 12**  *Second Sunday of Lent*

# Trashing the Temple

In the whole of the Bible, there is only one example of Jesus using physical violence on other people. That's the incident that we call "The Cleansing of the Temple."

It's utterly uncharacteristic of him.

In his temptations in the desert, Jesus specifically rejected any use of power—natural or supernatural—to accomplish his purposes. He would not *bribe* people into believing; he would not *awe* people into believing; and he would not *force* people into believing (Matthew 4:1–11; Luke 4:1–13).

Several times during his ministry, Jesus found himself in situations where he might well have been tempted to use physical force.

At least twice, his life was threatened. At Nazareth, the villagers of his own home town took him to the edge of a cliff, to stone him (Luke 4:28–30). Traditionally, a person executed by stoning was thrown over a cliff; then the two chief witnesses against that person had to dispatch the victim by smashing the first two boulders onto the broken body below. (Callous as it sounds, it ensured that people didn't spread malicious gossip idly—unless they had the stomach and conviction to finish off the job.) Perhaps, in this case, the villagers couldn't decide who would cast the first rock.

In any case, Jesus simply walked away.

Another time, in the Temple in Jerusalem, some Jews were apparently so outraged by Jesus' teaching that not once, but twice, they picked up stones to stone him (John 10:31, 39). But instead of retaliating, he "escaped from their clutches."

He explicitly rejected violence. When a Samaritan

town wouldn't receive him, James and John asked: "Do you want us to destroy them with fire from heaven?" Jesus rebuked them for even suggesting it, and went on to a different village (Luke 9:51–56).

Apparently, he got angry. One Sabbath, he was challenged to heal a man with a withered arm. If Jesus healed the arm, he would break the law. If he kept the law, he would act callously. The dilemma, for a devout and compassionate Jew, must have been agonizing. The people gathered around like vultures, waiting, watching, to see what he would do. The gospel of Mark (3:1–6) says that Jesus looked around him with anger. But he didn't act on that anger. He healed the man.

In fact, if you search through the gospels, you will find remarkably few instances of Jesus ever getting really angry. He felt sorrow, yes. Frustration, yes. Despair and pity and bone-weary exhaustion, yes. But rarely anger. And never anger with violence—except on this one occasion in the Temple.

We cannot simply attribute his action to shock, at seeing a holy place despoiled by crass commerce. Because it wasn't his first time in the Temple. The gospel of John suggests he had been there several times before—though John's chronology often disagrees with the other three gospels. But even according to the other gospels, this was not his first visit. He had been there at the age of twelve (Luke 2:41–52). His close friends—Mary, Martha, and Lazarus—lived in Bethany, a bedroom suburb of Jerusalem. That friendship suggests fairly frequent visits. And if he were near Jerusalem, he would certainly have visited the Temple, the centre of Jewish faith. In fact, it's hard to imagine him *not* having been in the Temple before, because every male Jew was expected to celebrate the Passover in Jerusalem (females didn't count in those days). Jesus may have reinterpreted the Jewish faith, but he was never apathetic about it. He was always a devout Jew.

Mark even says that he was in the Temple the evening before he attacked the traders. He looked around, and went away (Mark 11:11).

So what provoked him on this occasion?

I think he knew it would be his last chance to get across the message he had been preaching and living ever since he read the Scriptures in Nazareth—the time when he had almost been stoned. On that occasion, he went forward in the synagogue to read, a religious right of any male Jew.

The reading was not Jesus' choice. The Jews followed a strict lectionary—so strict that some scholars claim they can identify the precise day of the year this reading took place, from the passage selected. We can never know whether Jesus chose this particular day to go forward, knowing the passage he would be given, or whether the selected passage appeared by providential coincidence. Either way, he took the scroll, and began reading from his favorite prophet, Isaiah:

*The spirit of the Lord is upon me.*
*The Lord has appointed me...*
*to announce good news to the poor,*
*to proclaim release for the prisoners*
*and recovery of sight for the blind,*
*to let the broken victims go free,*
*to proclaim the year of the Lord's favor*(Isaiah 61:1-2).

From other references in the gospels, Jesus must have known Isaiah inside and out. Time and time again, he quotes a verse or a fragment of a verse from Isaiah. He alludes to images and metaphors from Isaiah in his parables. From Isaiah, Jesus got his model for the Messiah, the Suffering Servant. I wonder, sometimes, if his mother sang him the Psalms and read to him from the prophets at bedtime, the way our mothers told us Grimm's fairy tales and Mother Goose rhymes.

But he was not unique in knowing Isaiah—though certainly he understood and applied Isaiah's message uniquely to his life. Others would also find the reading familiar. So they would be startled when he didn't finish the reading. He didn't even finish the sentence—"and a day of vengeance for our God."

No wonder all eyes in the synagogue were fixed upon him! This local boy was taking unheard-of liberties with scripture.

Then Jesus opened his mouth. "Today," he said into the hushed silence, "this text has come true."

Many people take this passage as Jesus' political manifesto, his statement of purpose, a constitution for his ministry. It has become the definitive expression of what theologians call—in their typically impenetrable prose—"God's preferential option for the poor."

But if we read that passage as a statement of purpose, we would have to conclude that Jesus failed. He didn't release any captives. He didn't even free his own cousin John, beheaded by Herod during Jesus' ministry. There's no record of him setting any broken victims free.

Granted, he *did* announce good news to the poor. He *did* proclaim the year of the Lord's favor. And he *did* give sight to some blind people. But he certainly didn't end blindness. And in the end, he himself became one more prisoner, one more broken victim of a corrupt and oppressive political system.

Unless we link that statement of purpose with his action in the Temple.

By his last week, the heady excitement of the early days in Galilee had passed. More and more, he moved in an atmosphere of confrontation and heckling. Lawyers tossed him loaded questions, trying to trap him. They tested him on taxes, hoping his answer would alienate either the Romans or the rest of the Jews.

They even pitted his convictions against his compassion. For the Jews, adultery was a major offence. Adultery deserved the death penalty, for historic reasons. The Hebrew people had once been a nomadic tribe who depended on unflinching unity for their survival, in a hostile desert, among hostile neighbors. Nothing would destroy that unity more quickly than fooling around with someone else's wife or husband.

Jesus had already endorsed that historic law. In fact, he had gone beyond the law. He rejected divorce—which the law permitted. He had said that you committed adultery in your heart even by looking at a woman with lust (Matthew 5:27–28).

So what would he do, confronted with a woman caught in the act? She may have been caught legitimately. Or she may have been framed, used to set a trap for Jesus, perhaps even blackmailed into adultery by the power of the Temple priests. But however it happened, there was no question of her guilt (John 8:1–11).

The only question was how Jesus would react. The incident was stage-managed to create an impossible situation. As John describes the scene, while Jesus bent to write with his finger on the ground, the woman's accusers steadily taunted Jesus with questions.

Whenever that incident happened, it captures the tensions of his final week. In that atmosphere, only the most faithful—or perhaps the most pig-headed—of his disciples would hang on. And even they must have wondered if his commitment to releasing captives and freeing broken victims was just rhetoric, a politician's empty promises. They wanted to share Jesus' throne (Mark 10:35–40; Matthew 20:20–23), not his jail cell.

Jesus had to show them, somehow, that he really meant it. So he walked into the outer court of the Temple and started kicking over tables. He dumped the money-boxes, scattering cash. He flung open the cages, freeing the captive birds and animals.

And when the merchants and money changers fled, he refused to let them come back in! But he let the women and children in, and the blind and the crippled— the lowest levels of Jewish society. And the children sang songs and played games in the Temple yard, as if they had paid good rent for that space! (Matthew 21:14–16)

As an act of audacity, it compares to pulling the plug on Wall Street's computers and turning the Stock Exchange over to day care. To his terrified disciples, Jesus must have seemed suicidally inclined. They probably cowered in the corners, expecting the local SWAT team to appear over the walls at any moment...

But Jesus was right—those disciples didn't forget. It's one of the few incidents of his life that all four gospels include. Even the acts of the Last Supper, the foundation of all Christian worship and liturgy, don't make it into all four.

Three of those gospels put this incident in his final week; John's gospel puts the story of clearing the Temple at the beginning of Jesus' ministry. I prefer the majority version. Trashing the Temple seems an unlikely act with which to *begin* a ministry. It seems even less likely that, having trashed the Temple, Jesus would be allowed to hang around gathering followers, and even chatting with members of the ruling council. But it fits perfectly as a "last chance" act in Passion Week. It dramatizes, indelibly, the conviction he had shown all along for the poor, the outcasts, the sick, the lame, the blind, the women, the children.... It's the act of a man who has nothing more to lose.

Like choosing a donkey to ride on, trashing the Temple was a deliberate exception to his own rule, done to make a point. We make a mistake if we treat this incident as a model for our own action. Some Christians use it to justify violence against oppression. I think they're wrong. By taking an uncharacteristic incident out of context, they're just as guilty of proof-texting as those who can quote verses from the Bible to "prove" the validity of anything from child abuse to a flat earth.

Jesus had many other opportunities to combat evil and oppression with force. But he didn't. Why did he use force this time? Obviously, not to defeat the injustice. The merchants and money changers would be back before long, with armed guards. Rather, he did it to teach an unforgettable lesson.

His disciples recognized that, even if some of us don't. Read the records of their actions after Jesus' death. You'll find a great deal about universal sharing, about serving the weak and helpless, about speaking up for the underdogs. They healed the cripples, and accepted even the Gentiles. But you will find barely a word about the young church resorting to or condoning violence.

They learned the lesson Jesus was trying to teach them. Have we?

### Reading: Matthew 21:12–16
### Clearing the Temple

*Did you ever physically discipline your children?*
*Does that mean you support violence to solve problems?*
*Try to recall the incident. What did they do?*
*What were you trying to teach them?*

# Day 13 — Monday

Air Canada photo

I get nervous, flying. Not flying itself so much as taking off and landing. Not much can go wrong in level flight. It's much safer than driving a car, for example. No one is likely to rear-end the plane at a stoplight 10,000 feet up.

But every take off, every landing, has a point of no return, a moment when decisions become irrevocable. Even if a tire blows or an engine quits, the pilot has to continue. Past a certain point, there's no turning back. It's too late to change your mind....

I've wondered, sometimes, when Jesus passed *his* point of no return. At what point did the cross become inevitable?

Jesus had many opportunities to avoid crucifixion. During his trial, he might have denied being the Mes-

*LAST CHANCE*

siah. Before the trial, he could have slipped away to Bethany, or even back to Galilee, leaving Judas literally holding the bag. But he didn't. Clearly, in his own mind, he had passed the point of turning back.

Was it, perhaps, when the crowds thronged around him, shouting "Hosanna"? The authorities in Jerusalem saw his power, his charisma. They realized the kind of mass support he could generate.

Was it when he heard of the death of his friend Lazarus, and felt he had to come back to the dangerous territory of Judea? John's gospel (11:47-53) suggests that the point of no return came when Jesus raised Lazarus from the dead. "From that day on," says John, "the Jewish authorities made plans to kill Jesus."

Maybe. But both these "points of no return" have a common element. They involve some *external* factor—the crowd, the authorities, a friend's life. But in clearing the Temple, he acted on his own, decisively and deliberately. He didn't have to go on the rampage. Nobody demanded that he volunteer for demolition duty. And since he had seen the Temple the night before, it wasn't even spontaneous outrage.

But he did it. After that, it was too late to back out.

### Reading: Mark 11:11 & 15
### Looking around

*Before a big date, a job interview,
a marriage proposal, a mortgage application,
did you have to nerve yourself up?
Was it because you knew the answer could change your life?
What tasks do you have to nerve yourself up for these days?
What changes are you worried about?*

**Day 14**  *Tuesday*

Joan hates heights. Still, she agreed to go for a ride with the rest of our group of travellers on what's supposed to be the world's biggest ferris wheel, in Vienna.

The gondola, holding 20 or more people, swayed as it moved off. Though the gondola was completely enclosed, Joan hung onto the handrails so tightly that her knuckles went white.

"I'm afraid it might crash," she explained.

"How will holding on tight stop it from crashing?" I asked.

She looked at a friend, who was also hanging on for dear life. "We never thought of it that way," they replied together.

*The world's biggest ferris wheel—a long way off the ground!*

Hanging on tightly is a natural human reaction. While our daughter Sharon was learning to drive. I hung onto the armrest on the passenger's door. I almost pushed my foot through the floorboards. Yet I knew that neither action could have prevented an accident!

Sometimes we hang on to other things when we shouldn't. Like old ways, old habits.

So people cry out for the death penalty after a policeman's murder, even though the murderer immediately committed suicide. Clergy proclaim traditional family values to pews filled with the divorced, the re-married, and the never-married-but-living-with's. Capitalists and unions fight the battles of the 1920s.

Jesus didn't get rail against the Pharisees and the teachers of the law simply because they were doing wrong. In fact, they were probably the most rigorously righteous people of his time. They had a worthy aim. They wanted to protect and preserve the religious heritage of the Jewish faith. To avoid contamination by the culture of their time, they tried to govern even the smallest details of their lives by historic Hebrew laws and traditions.

But they hung on too tightly. They put law-and-order ahead of justice. They wouldn't allow God the privilege of doing something new, something different.

Sometimes we need to loosen our grip, too.

**Reading: Luke 11:37–46, 53–54
"Woe unto you…"**

*As a child, did you ever hide behind your mother's skirts
when a stranger visited?
When strange ideas call today,
what do you still try to hide behind?*

**Day 15**                                                              *Wednesday*

Government of India photo

A YWCA executive told me about a conference she attended in India.

As she arrived at her Bombay hotel, she recalled, "There was a woman on the sidewalk, near the front door, wailing a single high thin note. She never stopped in the three days we were there, other than to take a breath."

This woman came from a Third World nation herself. She knew about poverty and suffering; she knew about the unfairness of life. But that high thin endless wail of anguish unnerved her. She couldn't get away from it, even inside her comfortable hotel room, even when she tried to drown it out in the shower....

"For me, that sound will always be India," she said.

She made me more aware of sounds of societies.

In some parts of Africa, the most pervasive sound I heard was the dry scrape of hand hoes, wielded by women digging up sun-scorched stony ground to plant a few desperately needed crops.

In Rio de Janeiro, the snarl and roar of taxi drivers drag-racing away from every light—each determined to lead the pack, and the devil take the hindmost—reflected the city's survival-of-the-fittest ethic. The fortunate benefited from frantic growth, often at the expense of those being left behind.

In our own country, is the sound of a police or

ambulance siren shredding the darkness of the night the cry of a society in pain?

A bulldozer bellows its diesel song of power as it reshapes the earth; a truck blares by on the highway; a jet plane rattles windows as it takes off—is raw noise a symptom of our social arrogance?

Do we ever hear children singing in *our* temples to commerce?

**Reading: Matthew 18:1–7
Like a little child...**

*What sounds do you associate with your childhood?
With your work?
Your hobbies?
How many of those sounds
would you expect to hear in heaven?*

*Trashing the Temple*

**Day 16**                                               *Thursday*

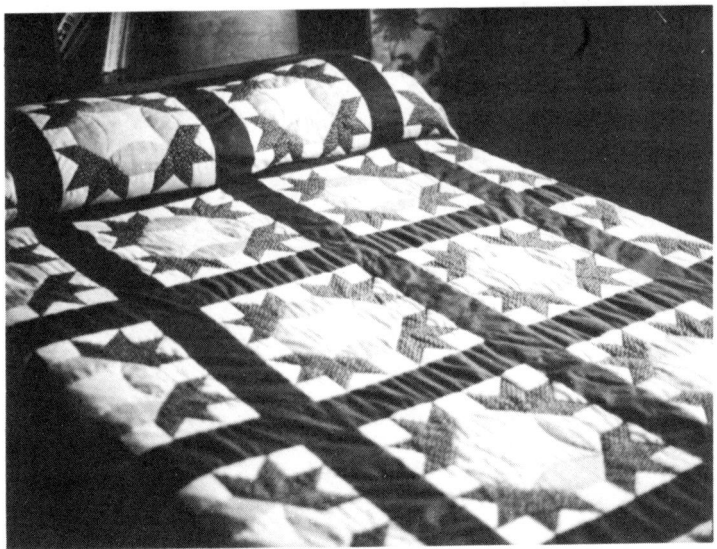

Joan makes quilts. Beautiful quilts. She puts a lot of work into them. But I didn't know how much they meant to her, until one summer when I made the bed wrong.

Because I work at home while Joan goes out to her office, I usually make the bed. During the summer, we don't sleep under the quilt. Nights are too hot in urban Toronto. So, to save myself some effort, I would leave the quilt folded at the foot of the bed.

One evening before supper, I caught Joan re-making the bed. Not the whole bed. Just stretching out the quilt and tucking it under the pillows the way she likes it done.

We had a furious argument. Silly as it sounds now, I thought she was belittling my ability—even my willingness—to make the bed. "Why does everything have to be done your way?" I ranted.

Somewhere in the middle of that battle, I suddenly realized how much that quilt mattered to her. She was proud of it, and she didn't want to see it hidden, all folded up at the bottom of the bed.

Some years ago, British author Mark Gibbs described the stages of evangelism—in fact, of *any* change, in *any* situation. In moving towards some consensus, he said, "you will have to get into a screaming bloody argument with each other." Not because you can change the other person's mind by "screaming." But because it's the only way you will ever hear what really matters to the other person.

He hastily added that we shouldn't go around *looking* for "screaming bloody arguments." We can too easily think that because we alienate people, we must be right—like artists who blame the public for not appreciating their art. The problem may lie with the art, not the public's taste.

But we shouldn't be ashamed of arguments, either. Getting that deeply involved shows that the subject matters to both sides enough to risk being vulnerable.

Jesus didn't clear the Temple to get rid of the traders. He cleared it to show that he was dead serious about what he said.

### Reading: Exodus 32:15–20
### Moses' temper tantrum

*Do you ever bottle up your anger?*
*Do you find yourself being polite to people you despise?*
*Or pretending to agree with policies you reject?*
*How does that help to solve the problem?*

# Day 17  Friday

One morning, back in high school, our home room teacher didn't show up.

We waited for someone to come and take attendance, and to send us off to our first class. No one came.

A few paper darts, pieces of chalk, and rubber bands flew through the air. Still no one came.

Someone suggested: "I think we should go to the other class anyway, even if Miss Skelton isn't here."

"Naw," said someone else. "You know how many times she's told us to wait until she dismisses us before we go to class."

"That's right," half a dozen people chimed in. "You know the rules." So no one moved.

A bit later, someone else repeated the suggestion. But still no one got up. We all sat, fidgeting, waiting for someone to make the first move.

Finally I could stand it no longer. "I don't care what the rules say," I blurted out. "And I don't care if you stay or not—I think I should go to that class."

I had no idea if anyone would come with me or not. At the door, I glanced back, expecting to be the only person on my feet, almost expecting to have to slink back to my seat in shame. To my astonishment, every member of the class was also moving towards the door.

I learned, that morning, that we can talk about an idea until water flows uphill, without changing a thing. Things change only when we take the risk of acting.

### Reading: Acts 10:17–29a
### Peter goes to a Gentile's home

*Think of someone you have been avoiding.*
*What do you dread about meeting them?*
*What's the worst that could happen if you see them?*
*Can you risk making the contact?*

**Day 18**　　　　　　　　　　　　　　　　*Saturday*

As a lecturer in sociology, Shirley Endicott worked with a group of battered wives. One husband tried to strangle his wife with the telephone cord; she escaped only because the telephone rang, and he stopped to answer it.

Shirley had thought—and taught—that wife beating happened mainly among lower-class families who didn't know any better. She was astounded to discover that it also happened among her university colleagues—and worse, that prevailing social attitudes condoned it. Not explicitly, of course. But implicitly. In sexist jokes, for example:

*"Do you you believe in clubs for women?"*
*"Only if persuasion fails."*

She began to realize that the "feminine" virtues taught to women—submissiveness, passivity, fidelity, patience, endurance—kept them in invisible chains, so that they couldn't break away from the very situation that threatened them.

Shirley described her experience this way, in her book *Facing the Tiger*:

"A flame of rage began to burn. I became a burning bush—the flame of rage burned but the bush did not burn up. This was unlike any anger I had felt before. Usually I would write a letter, make a phone call, sign a petition. Then the flame flickered and went out.... This was different..."

Maybe the significant fact in the story about Moses is not that he saw a burning bush, but that somehow he *became* a burning bush. Something out there in the desert lit a fire in him that would not go out. It drove him back to the land he had fled as a murderer; it impelled him into repeated confrontations with Pharaoh; it sustained him through 40 years in the wilderness.

Jesus knew that fire too, when he confronted the establishment of his time.

When contemporary prophets challenge entrenched attitudes, they won't fold their tents and creep away after setbacks either. They have a fire burning inside them that won't go out.

We keep studying the fire in the bush. We should study the fire in the person.

### Reading: Exodus 3: 1–4; 13:21–22)
### God as fire

*Which makes you more angry: an injustice done to you?*
*Or an injustice done to someone you love?*
*Which anger lasts longer?*
*If you can't get angry about something,*
*does that mean you don't care much about it?*

# Session Two

**Purpose**

This session challenges participants to consider how they themselves use or avoid violence in their lives.

**Preparation**

Everyone should have read Days 12-18 in the book.

Set up chairs so that people can see each other comfortably, as for Session One.

Draw a long line on the floor, or stretch a string across the floor, for use in the "Getting Involved" section.

**Getting started**

Open with prayer and/or singing.

Have any new members introduce themselves; those who participated in Session One should introduce themselves to newcomers. Even if no new members show up, have participants say a few words about their early childhood—where they lived, how big a family, what kind of discipline, etc.

**Getting involved**

Ask if the participants think violence is a good way to solve problems. But instead of answering in words, ask them to take a position on the line/string that corresponds to their views: way over at *this* end for those who think violence is *never* appropriate; way over at *that* end for those who think it may be the best way.

Invite selected people to explain why the stood where they did—or perhaps why they had trouble deciding where to stand.

Now ask how many have *never used violence themselves*—not even to deal with the neighborhood bully, nor to discipline children, nor to serve in the armed forces.... Find out why some of those who oppose violence may have used it.

**Starting the thoughts**

After participants have returned to their seats, present the concepts related to Jesus' actions in the Temple, as described in the reading for the 2nd Sunday of Lent. You may find one of the readings for the week, Days 13-18, or the questions related to one of the readings, helpful in grounding the theme in real life experiences.

(If you prefer, you may simply play the tape for this portion of the program.)

## Grounding thoughts in scripture

Read Luke 4: 16–19 together.

Have the group identify the kinds of people to whom this good news was addressed. Write the names on a flipchart: the poor, the captives, the blind, etc.

Find Matthew 21:12–16. Ask the group, as they read this parable aloud, to note who or what was being set free, given good news, etc., as listed on the flipchart. Read the passage together. Invite comments.

## Applying new understandings to life

Divide into smaller groups for discussion, if appropriate.

Assign three topics for discussion, depending on time available. (If you prefer, you may create your own questions, perhaps based on those with one or more of the daily readings.)

1. *When you read your newspaper or listen to the news, what kinds of things make you really angry?* Encourage people not only to reply factually, but to explain how they feel like reacting. What would they do to that person?

2. *Did you ever spank your children for hitting each other, or hitting someone else? What's the difference between your violence and theirs?* Younger or childless members may prefer to talk about their own experiences of being punished. How might, "to teach them a lesson," compare with Jesus' motives in cleansing the Temple?

3. Older members might recall the civil rights marches and protests of the '60s and early '70s, in Selma, Washington, Watts, Chicago.... *When, and why, did those protests and marches turn ugly and violent?*

## Putting it together

If you have divided into several groups for discussion, gather together again.

Invite participants to volunteer insights they may have gained during the discussion. (Sometimes one person will want to draw attention to an insight or discovery someone else seemed to have—that's quite acceptable.) Ask particularly about insights related to the use of violence to resolve social and justice problems.

Avoid, if possible, a reporting by a leader of what groups discussed.

## Closing

End with prayer, music if appropriate, and a blessing or benediction.

**Day 19**  *Third Sunday of Lent*

# Putting a person first

That final week was not all dramatic action. There were also quiet times, and sightseeing, and a lot of talking. The three gospels of Matthew, Mark, and Luke put most of the talking in the days *before* the Last Supper; John, who either had a fantastic memory or took shorthand, puts the longest speeches *after* the Supper.

Jerusalem was the centre of the Jewish universe, like Mecca to the Muslims. And Jerusalem during the Passover would be at its busiest and most exciting. The disciples were mostly unsophisticated country bumpkins from the backwoods of Galilee. Like tourists anywhere, they probably gawked at the Roman fortress, the historic tombs, the palaces. They wandered down streets thick with souvenir sellers—the city may have been much smaller then than it is now, but in Jerusalem, street vendors remain the same yesterday, today, and forever!

On their arrival, the first evening, they'd have stared at the magnificent Temple on its huge platform, towering over the huddled houses, gleaming in the glow of the setting sun.

Knowing that his time was growing short, Jesus took advantage of every possible "teaching moment"— every opportunity to get his message across.

So when he saw a poor widow, going up to place her pitiful offering in the treasury at the Temple, he turned her action into one of those teaching moments (Mark 12:41–44; Luke 21:1–4). Seeing her, says Mark's gospel, "he called his disciples together," so that he could use her as an example.

Similarly, when his disciples admired the architecture of the Temple—seemingly so permanent, so indestructible—he turned their naïve enthusiasm into a lesson about human nature and the ultimate reign of God. "For nation will rise against nation..." he cautioned. "Not one stone here will be left in its place; every one of them will be thrown down! ... But no one knows when that day or hour will come...." (Matthew 24:1-3, 6-7, 36; Mark 13:1-4, 7-8, 32; Luke 21:5-7, 9-11).

Even the city itself became an opportunity to make a point. Coming over the Mount of Olives from Bethany, seeing the city spread out below him in the clear morning sun, he lamented, "Oh, Jerusalem, Jerusalem... how I have wanted to gather your children, as a hen gathers her chicks under her wings...." (Matthew 23:37-39; Luke 13:34-35).

The last week in Jerusalem also produced a flood of parables. Short of the Sermon on the Mount (which, according to Luke, was neither on a mount, nor as long as Matthew makes it!), Passion Week gives us the richest lode of teachings in the Gospels, culminating in the Parable of the Sheep and the Goats (Matthew 25:31-46).

If the conversation about the greatest of the commandments, to "love God... and your neighbor as yourself," came during this week—as Matthew (22:34-40) and Mark (12:28-31) place it—then the parable of the Good Samaritan (Luke 10:25-37) may also belong to this week.

Luke places the Good Samaritan—like a number of teachings and incidents that other gospels include in the final week—elsewhere in Jesus' ministry. But Luke also gives a different context for many of the teachings that Matthew lumped together into the Sermon on the Mount. And we have no way of knowing—so long after the actual events—which chronology is most correct.

But the question about "the greatest of the commandments" sounds like the kind of constant testing that the Jerusalem lawyers subjected Jesus to, during that final week. And both the parables of the Good Samaritan and the Sheep and the Goats vividly illustrate the meaning of "loving your neighbor...."

Unfortunately, the disciples missed the point of these parables—whenever they were told. They almost got it. But not quite.

An incident in Bethany, where Jesus stayed at night, reveals that. Jesus had gone to the house of Simon the Leper for dinner. And as he sat there, a woman—John identifies her as Mary, the sister of Martha (John 12:1-8)—brought some expensive ointment, worth a whole year of a laborer's wages, and poured it on his head (Matthew 26:6-13; Mark 14:3-9).

For a tired man, tense after the constant confrontation in Jerusalem, grieving over the ever-shortening number of days of life left, the touch of that woman's hands must have felt wonderful. Perhaps she rubbed the warm oil into his scalp, and let it run down his neck, and gently kneaded the knotted muscles of his shoulders until they relaxed....

Perhaps, too, the disciples thought they were finally getting a grasp of their leader's goals. In the synagogue at Nazareth, he had formally declared himself on the side of the poor, the handicapped, the imprisoned, the oppressed. He had dramatically driven that message home in the Temple by turfing out the merchants and traders—those who exploited the devotion or ignorance of visitors to the Temple—and by freeing their captives. He had talked and eaten and partied with tax collectors and prostitutes and lepers—whom the good folks of Israel avoided the way we avoid people with AIDS. And finally, the Parable of the Sheep and Goats told them, in unmistakable language, to help those who didn't have clothes, or health, or homes, or even water.

*Putting a person first*

So they probably expected Jesus to praise them when they grumbled: "What a waste! If that lavish ointment had been sold, look how much we could have given to the poor!"

They fell into the same trap as most of us fall into. They thought about "the poor" generically. The lower classes. The great unwashed masses. A sea of faces needing help.

But Jesus never visited "the poor," nor talked with "the masses." He visited *people*. People he liked. People he knew personally. People he enjoyed being with.

Many people today give generously to support clothing stores and soup kitchens. But they wouldn't dream of getting to know a transient personally. They'll fund a hostel for battered wives, but they won't take abused women into their homes. They make compassion a *principle*; Jesus always made it a *person*.

We shouldn't judge the disciples harshly. Their own scripture instructed them, over and over, to look after strangers, widows, orphans, and other poor or underprivileged people among them. (e.g. Exodus 22:21–27). But their scriptures didn't say anything about *liking* those unfortunate people.

Still, their protest must have come as a shock to Jesus. Would they ever get it right? How many more chances did he have to get his understanding of God's nature across to them?

So Jesus quickly turned the incident into another teaching moment. "Leave her alone," he said to the disciples. "She has done a beautiful thing to me...."

This incident affected the disciples powerfully enough to appear in all four gospels. There are variations, of course. In Luke and John, the woman anoints his feet, not his head. In Luke, she uses her tears first, then the expensive ointment, and there's no squabble over squandered money. All four stories, however, happened in the house of someone named Simon. Luke describes him as a Pharisee, the other three as a leper. Possibly he was both. A leper who could maintain a house and invite dinner guests would have to be fairly influential.

Don't get distracted by the explanation attributed to Jesus in the versions of the story told by Matthew and John—that the woman was symbolically anointing Jesus' body before his burial. That concept must have come later. It would not make sense to the disciples until days—even weeks—after the incident. It was a new idea—and in that desperate final week, Jesus wasn't trying to introduce any *new* ideas. He simply wanted to hammer home the ideas he had *already* tried to get across to them.

Ignore, too, any symbolism of anointing a king. "Thou hast anointed my head with oil," says the familiar line of the 23rd Psalm. The notion of anointing a king comes from later Christian commentators, squeezing every triumphal drop of symbolism out of every possible incident. None of the gospels liken this incident to anointing a king. And Jesus, who repeatedly rejected the Superman model for the Messiah, would never have suggested it to his disciples.

Luke, I think, best catches the meaning of this dramatized parable. He avoids distraction by separating the incident entirely from the events of Passion Week (Luke 7:36–50).

In Luke's story, Jesus makes his point unmistakable. The woman was living, according to Luke, "an immoral life." But Jesus said: "Her great love proves that her many sins have been forgiven; *where little has been forgiven, little love is shown.*"

Love. Forgiveness. That was the point the disciples missed. You can't love as a duty; you can't forgive a

*Putting a person first*

principle. You can only love a *person*. You can only forgive a *person*.

Despite our good intentions, our support for relief programs, our struggle for justice, we often make the same mistake as the disciples did. We are to give "the least of these" our cold water, our clothes, and our company, not out of duty or obligation, but out of love. Similarly, we forgive them for whatever they may have done that was wrong, or foolish, or stupid, just as we have been forgiven for our own wrong, foolish, or stupid acts.

That is how to love our neighbors. As ourselves.

Even a woman of questionable morals.

Even "the least of these...."

### Reading: Mark 14:3–9
### The anointing of Jesus

*Have you ever given someone a gift you couldn't afford?*
*Did the giving make you feel good? Or resentful?*
*How would you have felt*
*if you got criticized for making that sacrifice,*
*for doing something generous, out of love?*

# Day 20                                                        *Monday*

When I play back my telephone answering machine, I often hear nervous coughs or throat-clearings. Then a voice says, "Well, I, er, that is..." and hangs up in confusion. I can understand that. It's not natural for humans to talk to machines.

Sometimes I get a different response. The phone rings. "Hello!" I say as cheerfully as I can manage. There's a long pause. Then the person on the other end says, "Is that really you? I expected your machine..."

I reassure them. Another pause. "I had my message all ready, but getting a real person has put it right out of my mind," the caller stammers sheepishly.

The first time that happened, I shrugged if off. But it has happened several times, with several people. I begin to discern a pattern. If it's disconcerting to get a machine when you expected a person, it's just as disconcerting to get a person when you expected a machine.

Often, our good works treat people like machines. We turn them into objects by calling them "recipients" or "refugees," "clients" or "victims." We hand out soup or old clothing, and expect automatic gratitude. We're startled—even upset—to encounter people who have pride, who get angry, who want us to listen.

Jesus always recognized the person behind the blindness, the disease, the disability. Do we?

### Reading: Luke 18:35-43
### A blind man demands attention

*Jean Vanier once said: "The point is not whether you have a car, but who may ride in it. Not if you have a refrigerator, but who may eat from it." Would you let the recipients of your good will ride in your car, eat from your refrigerator, share your life? Would you rather have them stay objects?*

*Putting a person first*

# Day 21                           *Tuesday*

The massive pillars of the cathedral soared to a distant roof. We craned our necks in awe, staring heavenwards to its vaulted ceilings. Stained glass windows splashed the interior with color. Carvings of stone, of wood, of ivory, testified to the artistry of anonymous creators. Gold leaf gleamed on its altars.

The builders of this cathedral had lavished great wealth upon it.

Yet this ornate, opulent cathedral had been built by stone masons working for pennies a day, or less. Its luxury came from the contributions of uneducated, illiterate peasants, serfs owned like slaves by feudal landlords, eking out a desperate living in squalid huts, dying of the plague, of smallpox, of tuberculosis....

"It's magnificent," breathed one tourist.

"It's disgraceful!" spluttered another. "Those poor devils—think how much better off they would have been, if all that energy and money had been used to improve their education or their hygiene, instead of on this... this monument to human aspiration."

Suddenly we saw the cathedral with different eyes. Only a corrupt and self-serving church could demand such sacrifices of the poor and powerless, we thought.

"This could have been better spent on the poor," the disciples protested, when Mary squandered expensive ointment on Jesus. But Jesus disagreed: "It is a fine and beautiful thing that she has done for me," he replied.

It was a fine and beautiful thing, too, that the serfs and peasants of that long-ago city created.

Had all that cost and energy been spent on themselves, they might have lived a little longer, a little easier. But if they had the choice, would they rather have in their midst a cathedral that soared over them, reflecting their hopes and aspirations? Or a dozen extra days of mortal life?

Instead of a few days, they gained a sliver of immortality. Centuries later, their cathedral still stands. It still testifies, to stunned visitors, the builders' convictions that the chief aim of humankind was to worship and glorify God.

### Reading: Matthew 26:6–13
### The woman at Bethany

*As a child, did you prefer practical gifts like socks or shirts?*
*Or impractical ones that invited you*
*to adventure, to fantasy?*
*Have you changed all that much?*
*Has God?*

*Putting a person first*

**Day 22**  Wednesday

Wolf Kutnahorsky/Berkeley Studio photo

The Chinese tell a folk-tale about the Great Wall of China.

Thousands of laborers died building the wall. Their bodies were tossed inside the wall, to be entombed by tons of rock.

The wife of one of these victims, a woman known as Lady Meng, went to the wall to retrieve her husband's bones, so that he might be properly buried. But when she saw the wall, its size, its solidity, its invulnerability, she knew she could do nothing.

So she sat down on the wall and wept. And her tears touched the wall, and dissolved its rigid mortar; it collapsed, and laid bare her husband's bones.

An Asian theologian, C. S. Song, told that story to the Christian Conference of Asia meeting in India. He talked about the power of tears. About how Jesus wept. About how survivors of the Kwangju massacre in Korea wept for their lost sons and husbands, wept as they took up the struggle themselves. About how useless tears are, and how necessary.

And he talked about people who can no longer cry, because they no longer have any hope to cry for.

"Tears mean the capacity for love," said Song. "Through our tears, we may still keep this world human and divine. That is why people must not run out of tears."

For those who value practicality, tears are useless. They reveal weakness. They accomplish nothing. Weeping is an act of vulnerability, of helplessness. No one, while sobbing one's heart out, can at the same time guard against a potential knife in the back, or watch for opportunities to move ahead...

Yet Lady Meng's tears moved even the greatest of walls, and it collapsed.

We underestimate the power of tears.

### Reading: Luke 7:36–38, 44–47
### Washing Jesus' feet

*Is the ability to cry a sign that you can still hope?*
*If you won't let yourself cry,*
*do you still let yourself hope?*

# Day 23 — Thursday

Fr. Frank Hegel wrote in the Scarboro Foreign Mission Society magazine about his work with "street kids" in South America. His city has rich history, past culture, former splendour—but terrible poverty in the present. Here's how Hegel described one of those kids:

"He was lying face down on the sidewalk, a bundle of skin and bones, covered with dirty clothes. His skin had turned a frightening, unnatural yellow... He hadn't eaten for three days, and had been chain-smoking pitilles—cigarettes laced with bad quality coca paste containing kerosene, caustic soda and sulphuric acid...."

Hegel described arriving at the local market with a colleague. They were tackled, he said, by "a mad dash of about a dozen children, some dressed in nothing more than their undershorts, their bodies filled with scars from cuts and burns and bruises. Shouting excitedly, they literally fought to climb up our bodies... Those who didn't make it clung tightly to our legs, arms or waists...."

That kind of world seems totally foreign to me. But Hegel's diagnosis of the problem hits almost too close to home. The kids' problem goes beyond food, or clothing, or even shelter: "Have you ever tried to convince someone who has never experienced love that, in reality, they are loved? It seems so simple, but it really isn't. Despite the work that we do with these children, there remains in the children a certain degree of mistrust and doubt. They've been hurt too often, and are fighting against all odds not to be hurt again."

How do you convince someone they're loved? I watched an evangelist working his television audience. "Jesus loves you," he kept telling the camera lens. "Jesus loves you."

But people in North America have been hurt too often, too; like the South American street kids, they don't want to be hurt again either. How are they going to know that Jesus loves them? Who's going to show them?

Not the man on the television tube. When his hour is over, he's gone out of their lives.

To overcome that lingering "degree of mistrust and doubt," the evidence has to come from other people. From the cashier at the supermarket. The taxi driver. The shop steward. The tax accountant. The used car seller.

From you and me.

### Reading: Matthew 25:32-45
### The sheep and the goats

*We've all let someone down, some time.*
*But did you ever think that your failure*
*might reflect the kind of God you claim to worship?*
*Even more important—did they?*

**Day 24**  *Friday*

When I was younger, humiliation or anger could reduce me to tears. As I grow older, I find myself moved to tears more often by tenderness, gentleness, and caring.

To conclude a weekend event at Kew Beach United Church, participating families led the Sunday morning worship service. One family sticks in my mind—a mother, a father, a son, and a young girl with Down's Syndrome. The girl was obviously a handful, and at times a strain. During the weekend, she had demonstrated that she didn't always take kindly to discipline or instruction. Still, they included her when they came forward to lead the prayer of dedication for the offering.

Both of the parents and the boy said thier prepared sentences. Then they held the microphone down, to give the girl the last word.

Most of us, I suspect, had our hearts in our mouths. A couple of times over the weekend, she had simply taken the microphone and shouted nonsense syllables into it, just to hear her own voice amplified.

She took the microphone.

"Amen," she said, clearly and precisely.

And she squeezed her mother's hand.

Long ago, the prophet Isaiah offered his people a vision of the Peaceable Kingdom:

*The wolf will live with the lamb,*
*the leopard will lie down with the goat,*
*the calf and the lion and the yearling together,*
*and a little child will lead them...*
*The infant will play near the hole of the cobra,*
*and the young child put its hand in the viper's nest.*
*They will neither harm nor destroy*
*on all my holy mountain...*

Of all the pictures to grace the cover of *National Geographic*, none stands out in my memory like the one of a gorilla cradling a tiny tabby kitten in its hairy black

arms. Isaiah would recognize his vision in that gorilla, so powerful, so mighty, cuddling a kitten.

I think Isaiah would recognize his vision in a woman rubbing sweet-smelling ointment into a desperately tired man's scalp, too.

Perhaps that's what moves me to tears—the recognition that in moments of tenderness and gentleness, I glimpse, for a moment, the way God meant the world to be.

### Reading: Isaiah 11:1–9
### A vision of hope

*Isaiah saw a world of predators and victims.*
*In today's world, who are the wolves? Who are the lambs?*
*How could you shape your corner of the world,*
*to help them live together in peace and harmony?*

**Day 25**               *Saturday*

A few years ago, three generations of us gathered around a picnic table, with the sun shining on us, the mountains towering above, the river rolling by, a soft breeze shimmering the leaves of the trees....

At such moments, I sense that this is the way the world was supposed to be.

Isn't that essentially what we celebrate in worship—that instinctive, involuntary recognition that "This is how things should be"? We gather up those best times, and we act them out to say, "This must be what life with God is like."

Granted, not all families are happy. Some babies are born to abuse and suffering, and some marriages exploit partners. But still we yearn for what a family can be—that gathering of people who each have different qualities and needs, who are unequal and yet who all equally contribute to the well-being and welfare, the health and wholeness, of the community called a family. So in our baptismal liturgies, the person entering the church—whether as adult or infant—passes symbolically through the waters of the womb and is born again into the family of God.

Not all fathers are kind. (Or all mothers, for that matter.) But still we know what fathers at their best can be like. And so for 20 centuries we have followed Jesus' example in calling God "Father."

Nor are all meals happy. Quarrels can be carried to the dinner table. Food can be an instrument of power, of division, of oppression. But somehow, when families gather for Christmas or Thanksgiving dinner, when church people gather in friendship for an anniversary or a potluck supper, we sense that this is how it should be, for everyone, everywhere. Then we act out that conviction symbolically when we share the bread and the wine in the Lord's Supper.

In these occasions, we catch and we enact a glimpse of *Shalom*, the way God wants the world to be.

### Reading: John 2:1–11
### A shared celebration

*What would the world be like,*
*if everyone treated you as a friend?*
*Could you help that happen,*
*if you treated everyone as a friend?*

*Putting a person first*

## Session Three

(Note that this session may be skipped if necessary)

**Purpose**
The theme of this session is that we can't "do good" out of principle or duty; we need to consider and care about the needs of the receivers as individuals.

**Preparation**
Every participant should read Days 19-25 in the book.
Set up chairs and other facilities as necessary
Have some blindfolds ready for use.

**Getting started**
Open with prayer, and/or singing.
Ask for a few volunteers—just a few—to prove a point. Suggest that in our society we pay considerable attention with our *eyes* and our *ears*, but not very much with *other senses*. Then blindfold the volunteers. Invite an equal number of other volunteers, preferably people well known to the blindfolded volunteers—to sit absolutely silently on a row of chairs. See how long it takes a blindfolded volunteer to identify a seated volunteer, by touching only the face and head.

As a second, or alternate, method, invite paired spouses or close friends to stand back to back, so that they can't see each other. Then have one try to describe what the other one is wearing!

**Getting involved**
Brainstorm the qualities of good teachers that participants remember from their own school days. What made those teachers good? Fill a flipchart with ideas from the group: their personality, their relationship with students, their willingness to diverge from set lesson plans to base a lesson on recent news or current events, willingness to listen, to discuss, etc.

When you have enough on the flipchart, draw attention to as many qualities as possible that deal with a teacher taking advantage of natural opportunities and caring about the students as individuals.

**Starting the thoughts**
Present the ideas in the reading for Day 19, the 3rd Sunday in Lent. In this session particularly, it may be helpful to illustrate the point with some of your own personal experiences. Or draw upon the stories of Days 20–25 to supplement the main theme.

Emphasize two points particularly:
- One, that during this last week, Jesus took every incident as an opportunity to teach.
- Two, that in giving, the needs of the receiver matter far more than the principles of the giver.

(Or, if you prefer, play the tape for this portion of the program.)

### Grounding thoughts in scripture

Draw attention to, even if you don't read in full, the wealth of parables that Jesus apparently taught in that last week. Follow the parables through in Matthew's gospel, chapter 21-25, indicating the parallels in Mark and Luke.
- Matthew 21:28–32, The Two Sons
- Matthew 21:33–43, The Tenants in the Vineyard (also Mark 12:1–12, Luke 20:9–19)
- Matthew 22:1–14, The Wedding Feast, (Also Luke 14:16-24)
- Matthew 24:32–33, The Fig Tree (also Mark 13:28–29, Luke 21:29–31)
- Matthew 24:42–44, The Watchful Householder (also Luke 12:39–40)
- Matthew 24:45–51, The Faithful Servant (also Luke 12:42–46)
- Matthew 25:1–13, The Ten Maidens
- Matthew 25:14–30, The Talents (also Luke 19:12–27)

End by reading together the parable of The Sheep and the Goats (Matthew 25:31–46). Ask participants to notice what was done for each person in need—what that person needed....

Now read Mark 14:3-9 together. Ask what Jesus needed at that moment. Who gave it to him: the woman, or the disciples?

### Applying new understandings to life

Divide into smaller groups as necessary. Discuss these questions, or others that you develop yourself.

1. *Do you ever feel guilty about how much you have?* Or, for some, perhaps, *Do you ever feel angry that others have much more than you do?* In either case, why?

2. *Do you feel more comfortable giving or receiving?* Encourage participants to give specific examples from their lives. Encourage them also to put themselves in the other person's position.

3. Look at the statement attributed to Jean Vanier, at the end of Day 22. *Whom do you allow to eat from your refrigerator, or to ride in your car? What restrictions do you put on other uses of your property?* Do we, as givers, prefer that the recipients of our generosity remain "anonymous "objects"?

**Putting it together**

If you have divided into several groups for discussion, gather together again.

Invite participants to volunteer insights they may have gained during the discussion. What difference, if any, will this evening's discussion make to their charitable givings and activities?

Avoid, if possible, a reporting of what groups discussed.

**Closing**

End with prayer, music if appropriate, and a blessing or benediction.

**Day 26**  *Fourth Sunday of Lent*

# The servant savior

When the disciples objected to the woman's unthinking generosity, in Bethany, Jesus realized how close his disciples could come to understanding his message without quite getting it right. Just in case the point still had not yet penetrated their minds, he set them an example they could never forget.

He had to flush out of their minds any lingering thoughts of the Messiah as a conquering hero, rallying Jewish zealots against external foes. His followers had to recognize, for all time, that they were not to be a privileged élite doing good to the less fortunate.

So Jesus shocked them by assuming the role of a servant. Or—perhaps even more startling in that patriarchal society—the role of the sinful woman who had washed his feet with her tears.

He washed their feet.

This action, I'm convinced, most clearly illustrates his intention for that final week—*to teach* his disciples. Up to this point, Jesus' enacted parables, his dramatized teaching moments, had been accessible to anyone present. Large crowds had watched his entry to Jerusalem. He had taught daily in the Temple (Luke 21:37–38). The Temple was always busy; during Passover, it would be packed. He attracted both seekers of enlightenment and entertainment; the persistent heckling of the Jewish religious establishment would provide lively listening.

Even out at Bethany, on the far side of the Mount of Olives, outsiders heard him. According to some old traditions, Jesus' mother Mary came to the house in Bethany during that final week to say goodbye to him. The dinner at Simon the Leper's had at least the host and the woman present, as well as the disciples.

But at the Last Supper in the upper room, he had no audience but his disciples. Not even servants were present. So he can have aimed his message *only* at those few who would soon have to carry on without him.

To capture their attention, he acted first, explained later. Without saying a word, he took a towel, wrapped it around his waist like an apron, poured some water into a basin, and started washing their feet (John 13:1–15).

Feet, in dusty desert countries, get very dirty. Sandals protect feet from the worst of sharp rocks. But sandals can't compare with modern hiking boots or running shoes for comfort. Those sandals were little more than a single thickness of leather held to the bottom of feet by thongs or straps. So feet got tired. As an act of common courtesy, hosts washed their guests' feet.

Of course, the hosts themselves didn't do it. Washing dirty, smelly feet was a menial task that no one of any social standing would lower himself to doing. The task was normally assigned to servants or a slaves—who presumably had no delicate sensibilities. In homes without servants or slaves, a wife or daughter might provide the service.

But the upper room had no servants. And none of the twelve wanted to demean himself by taking a servant's role. Perhaps they still thought of honored positions in the coming kingdom (Matthew 20:20–28; Mark 10:35–45; Luke 22:24–27). When James and John had requested special privileges, Jesus had told them: "Whoever must be first among you must be the slave of all." But they obviously hadn't understood.

Jesus could have lectured them, as he had so many times before. But he didn't. He was their host; he became their servant.

Despite their shock, the water and towel must have

felt good—perhaps almost as good as the perfumed oil the woman had used on Jesus at Bethany.

If Jesus intended to provide a memorable experience, he certainly succeeded. As he moved from person to person, the disciples must have stared wild-eyed at each other over the figure kneeling at their feet. Until impetuous Peter could no longer contain himself. If I may paraphrase him loosely, he burst out: "Lord, what the hell do you think you're doing washing our feet?"

The vehemence of his words—even in the decorous language of most Bibles—attests to his involvement.

Jesus told Peter: "Unless I wash them, you can't be my disciple." Or, perhaps more colloquially: "My way, or no way!"

Then he did no more teaching until he had finished, until he had dressed and returned to his place at the table. By that time everyone was personally involved; everyone's feet had been bathed and dried.

Only then did he speak: "Do you understand what I have done for you?" he asked. "If I, your teacher and leader, have been willing to wash your feet, you should also be willing to wash one another's feet. I have set you an example...."

We have no way of knowing if this story happened *exactly* as the Bible relates it. It's told in only one gospel, the one attributed to John, the "disciple whom Jesus loved best." Most of the powerful events, the dramatized parables, had such an impact that all four gospels reported them. But this story appears in only one.

Personally, I believe it. But to back up my belief, I have to go on a fairly long digression.

Biblical scholars agree—as far as biblical scholars agree on anything—that John took a few liberties with the story of Jesus' life. John's was the last account of Jesus' life, written some 60 or 70 years after the events it describes. Mark's version of the incidents introduced the story of Jesus to strangers; Matthew's treated Jesus as the fulfillment of ancient Jewish prophecy, for those steeped in Jewish tradition; Luke's emphasized that Jesus' message was for Gentiles as well as Jews. By the time of John's gospel, Christianity was already a fairly well-established religion. In half a century, it had developed some of its own internal variations. John wrote not so much a history as a theological treatise, to correct the misunderstandings of some growing sects.

So John says things that the other gospels do not. The other three, for example, all indicate that Jesus avoided identification as the promised Messiah until the final days. That's reasonable; Messiahs tended to have relatively short lives. The Messiah, in the common understanding, claimed to be a descendent of David entitled to rule the Hebrew people. Some Messiahs gathered a band of foolhardy followers, launched a revolution, and got wiped out in a battle. The authorities exterminated others before they seriously threatened law and order. Herod massacred a whole village of infants, to prevent any of them from ever contesting his throne (Matthew 2:16–18). So Jesus might naturally prefer *not* to have his status widely proclaimed. But John asserts that from the very beginning—indeed, even from the beginning of creation—Jesus was the Savior, the promised one. And he insists that this *should have been clear to everyone*—although, of course, it wasn't.

In other variations, John puts the cleansing of the Temple at the beginning of Jesus' ministry; the others put it at the end. John deals mostly with incidents in and around Jerusalem; the others deal mostly with Galilee. John refers to three visits to Jerusalem at Passover time; the others mention only one.

John may also have taken some liberties with Jesus'

words. If the writer of the fourth gospel was indeed the disciple John, he and the other disciples—in those first frantic days of the church—would have gone over everything that Jesus had said and done, time and time again, trying to make sense out of it. Many times, one of them must have said: "Aha! *Now* I see what he was getting at!"

Some of those flashes of insight John incorporated into his gospel, as if Jesus himself had said the words. Such messages would carry much more authority coming directly from the Messiah than as a later amendment by a self-confessed slow-learner.

Besides, putting words in someone else's mouth wasn't considered deception in those days. Plato attributed most of his ideas to his teacher, Socrates. No one objected; no one felt cheated.

So several of Jesus' discourses—particularly his long speech after the Last Supper itself—may be not so much what Jesus actually said, as what the disciples became convinced he was trying to say to them.

I don't think that any of this invalidates John's gospel. Even if some of the words attributed to Jesus were not actually *uttered* by him, who could better interpret his intent than his closest friends? First hand witnesses—especially witnesses who have struggled to reach a consensus—are far more dependable than second-hand guesswork.

But there's another reason why I trust the accuracy of John's *incidents*, even if I have reservations about his *chronology*. As Dorothy L. Sayers pointed out in her preface to *The Man Born to Be King*, the incidents narrated in John have a ring of authenticity. When dramatizing incidents from the other gospels into the radio plays broadcast by the BBC as *The Man Born To Be King*, she had to add lines to make the dialogue believable. But John's stories could be used almost word-for-word.

"It is John," Sayers writes, "who remembers not only what Jesus said, but what others said to him... It is John who faithfully reproduces the emphasis and repetition of a teacher trying to get a new idea across... Indeed, when John is the authority for any scene, the playwright's task is easy. .... All through, in fact, the Gospel of St. John reads like the narrative of an eye-witness filling up the gaps in matter already published, correcting occasional errors, and adding material which previous writers either had not remembered or did not know about."

My final reason for accepting this story as true is that it fits. It substantiates Jesus' previous teachings; it corresponds to his character; above all, it continues that style of teaching he adopted for his final days.

As a dramatized parable, too, it worked. After that meal, Jesus had no further opportunities to teach about the role of a servant leader. Nor did he need one. The book of Acts tells us that the early church had no hierarchy, no one in positions of superiority. They shared all that they had, with anyone in need. When any accusations of favoritism arose, the church moved to remedy the situation (Acts 4:32–35; 6:1–7).

They finally got the message—just in time.

### Reading: John 13:3–15
### Washing the feet

*Have you ever taken second best—the moldy muffin,*
*the broken pie, the crumbled cookie—*
*so that someone you loved could have a better share?*
*Did you think of it as servant leadership, like washing feet?*
*Did you feel good about it?*
*Or resentful?*

# Day 27 — Monday

Imagine driving along a rocky coast, and seeing a battered old outhouse, perched out on the rocks at the end of a point jutting into the sea, .

When most people first see such an outhouse, they usually regard it with some amusement. Unless they feel some need for it. Then they turn to the outhouse with a kind of desperation. But as they hasten towards it, they make a few discoveries.

The way is not as easy as it looks. The route is rough. It tends to upset you and land you right on your... umm, well, that is, it tends to upset your equilibrium.

The closer you get to your destination, the fewer routes you have available for reaching it. Your choices narrow. The multitude of paths that you are accustomed to taking through life gets increasingly restricted by the presence of the sea pressing in on you on both sides of the rocky point.

When the disciples first started to follow Jesus, they had many options—including quitting and going back to their former occupations. But as time passed, as their commitment grew, their choices narrowed too. They could no longer drop out. Yet it got harder and harder to continue.

And towards the end, they must have wondered if the goal deserved all that effort.

From a distance, the outhouse may look safe and solid. Close up, you can see all the flaws in it, including the cracks that let the bitter sea wind through. There's little security, little privacy. And the seat looks weather-beaten, even hazardous.

The disciples had expected that leadership would bring them prestige and privilege. The concept of leading through humility, through service to others, must have shocked them. They had originally expected thrones; during that final week, they must have thought

*The servant savior*

they they realized they were more likely to get splinters in their rears.

Still, once you're committed....

### Readings: Luke 13:24–27, 30.
### The narrow door

*If you're a parent, did you have any idea
what you were letting yourself in for,
when you decided to have children?
How did your rosy dreams compare with harsh realities?
But wasn't it worthwhile anyway?*

*More likely to get splinters...*

**Day 28**  *Tuesday*

Two wash-basins changed the world. One of them was probably silver, maybe even gold. The other was probably cheap pottery.

All we know is who used them—and that they really did change the world.

The cheap one was used to wash a dozen people's feet. On the night we call "The Last Supper," Jesus and his closest friends met for dinner. But there was no servant to wash people's feet. So Jesus took that cheap washbasin and washed their feet as if he were a servant.

Pilate, the Roman governor in Jerusalem, used the other basin. He lived in luxury and power. He could free people, or put people to death.

But when Jesus appeared before him, Pilate found he didn't have as much power as he thought. He couldn't find Jesus guilty of anything. Nor could he free him. In spite of his Roman legions, Pilate had to do what people expected of him.

Jesus, Pilate realized, was free to do things differently. So he sent Jesus to the cross. But first, he took his basin, and washed his hands in it, to show the world that he took no responsibility for what he was doing.

Many people still think the way to improve the world is to have power, so they can *force* people to be good. Fortunately, some people are willing to try Jesus' way of changing the world.

### Reading: Matthew 27:22-24
### Pilate refuses responsibility

*In a meeting, if a majority votes against you,*
*do you help the majority anyway?*
*Or do you opt out of further responsibility?*
*Which kind of washbasin are you using?*

From *An Everyday God*, pages 82–83.

*The servant savior*

**Day 29**  *Wednesday*

One September, I helped our daughter Sharon move into a new apartment at Queen's University, in Kingston, Ontario. It was on the third floor. By the time I got to the top of three flights of stairs with a load of her books, clothes, housewares, or furniture, I found myself gasping and wheezing.

I used to pride myself on keeping in good physical condition. I had no idea how sedentary a writer's life had made me.

The next morning, I started getting back into shape. I started jogging.

Jogging, I'm convinced, is a form of masochism—like owning British sports cars. You force your creaking muscles to carry you around your route so that tomorrow morning you can try to do it again. If you ever get to the point where you can run that distance easily, you have to create new agony by going faster or farther.

Aside from helping my body, jogging gave me a few minutes a day when neither the telephone nor the doorbell could interrupt my thoughts.

Jogging also helped me understand the subtle difference between penance and repentance—two very similar words that come from the same roots, but that are often confused.

It used to bother me, for example, when some nominally Roman Catholic acquaintances described going to confession, doing penance, and then considering themselves freed of their sin. Something in their attitude didn't make sense, but I wasn't sure what it was. Now I know.

Jogging is like doing penance. I go jogging to pay for too many hours spent sitting at a desk, for too many rich meals, and for driving the car to the corner store.

But penance is not repentance. Genuine repentance would mean getting more exercise through the day,

cutting down on candy, and walking to the store. Repentance requires change.

If I genuinely repented, I wouldn't have to go jogging every morning. Genuine repentance makes penance unnecessary.

**Reading: Matthew 27:3–5**
**Judas repents**

*Recall an occasion when you fought with a friend.*
*Did you both say "Sorry"?*
*Why? Just to cool the conflict?*
*Or did you really change?*

**Day 30**                                        *Thursday*

Our old cat Tuppence was 17 when she caught her last bird. At that age, she moved fairly slowly and had only one tooth. So I think she was as surprised as the sparrow she caught.

I heard her outside the back door, making that peculiar yowl that says: "See what I've brought you!"

The sparrow seemed minimally damaged. Its feathers were certainly ruffled, and it was in shock—but how much damage can one tooth do? I rescued it, smoothed its feathers, and set it out on the lawn.

It didn't fly away.

I watched from a distance to make sure that after I had saved it from one cat, it didn't fall prey to another.

But it didn't fly.

Almost an hour later, it still crouched on the ground. It stood a little taller, its eyes were brighter, and it moved its head to watch whatever was happening—but it still wouldn't believe it was free to fly away.

That silly sparrow didn't fly until I finally lost patience and flung it into the air.

I thought of that bird the night our Bible study group struggled with the opening chapters of Paul's letter to the church in Rome. "In the past," he said in essence, "you were prisoners of the law. But Christ has freed you. Why do you continue to be bound by the restrictions of the past?"

Somebody suggested that we should substitute "culture" for "law" in applying Paul's letter to ourselves. For we are often captives of our culture without realizing it, conforming to social norms and standards, slaves to the whims of marketing and merchandising. Christ gives us an alternate vision, a reference point from which we can see fad and fashion for what they are. Christ frees us from the domination of our culture.

Why then do we continue as captives of the values and standards of the world around us?

Like the sparrow, are we afraid to fly?

### Reading: Romans 3:20–24
### Freed by Jesus

*Have you recently turned down any opportunities
to try something new?
Like skin diving, or flower arranging...
or studying the Bible?
Were you afraid of looking foolish?
Are you afraid to fly?*

**Day 31**  *Friday*

For years, I was a Scout leader. Older Scouts eventually graduated to Venturers, a program which encouraged them to run their own activities. The leader was now called an "Advisor," not a "Scoutmaster." The boys elected their own executive each year, to organize camping trips, parties, and fund-raising events.

One year, they chose David Fugeman as president. David had a rough time. He came to me one day, almost in tears. "These guys just won't do what I tell them," he lamented.

As I asked a few questions, his attitudes about leadership came clearer. He had been chosen. Therefore, he didn't have to *do* anything any more. He issued commands, like royalty—those who had chosen him, presumably, had also chosen to obey.

"That's one form of leadership, I suppose," I said.

"What's another?" he asked, with a trace of desperation in his voice.

"Maybe having people *want* to do things your way."

"How do I do that?" he demanded.

"By setting an example," I suggested. "By showing them that you're willing to do everything you can for them, until they're willing to pitch in and help you."

He shrugged. "I'll try anything," he said.

And he did. David turned out to be one of the best presidents that group had had. Very few programs failed for lack of organization that year.

The disciples shared David's problem. Hadn't they been chosen by Jesus? Didn't that make them special?

Jesus tried to explain to them, just as the prophets had tried to tell Israel, God's chosen people, that they were chosen for responsibility, not privilege. He succeeded no better than the prophets had.

In the end, both Jesus and God had to *show*, instead of *tell*. Jesus *showed* the disciples what he meant, by washing their feet. At the same time, in Jesus, God *showed* all of us what humans could be.

**Reading: 1 John 4:7–21
The example to follow**

*Think back to your school days.
Which teachers do you remember most fondly?
The ones who told you what to learn?
Or the ones who helped you do your own learning?*

*Three of the Venturers on a camping trip*

*The servant savior*

**Day 32**  *Saturday*

During the final days of our son Stephen's life, he was so weak that he could only cough in slow motion. He had no strength left to expel the mucus clogging his lungs. We three—his mother, his sister, and I—took turns rubbing the muscles of his chest and back to help him relax, so that he could breathe a little easier.

By normal standards, no one would have considered Stephen beautiful. Beautiful is Sophia Loren or Robert Redford. Stephen had once stood more than six feet tall, but now his back was stooped and hunched. He weighed no more than 90 pounds—so skinny his arms and legs looked like Tinkertoy with knobs for the elbows and knees. He had the body of an Auschwitz survivor...But after years of struggling to compensate for chronic lung congestion, he had developed an enormous barrel chest. It swelled over the rest of his shrivelled body like a mushroom over its stalk.

Gently, I rubbed his bony shoulder blades. With my finger tips, I massaged strands of muscle in his back. And as I stroked his skin, I found myself thinking that he had a beautiful body. Not beautiful because it was perfect. But beautiful because I loved it.

By those same normal standards, rubbing his chest was a futile exercise. He died less than 24 hours later. I was doing a meaningless ritual, a mindless task for a servant, something that had no value—

Except to him, and to me.

Nothing else has ever felt so worthwhile.

### Reading: Luke 5:12–13
### Touching a leper

*Do you find changing a baby's dirty diaper repugnant?*
*Or a celebration of love?*
*Does it make any difference whose baby you're changing?*

# Session Four

**Purpose**

This session focuses on Jesus' actions in taking a servant's role and washing his disciples feet, and the implications of that action if we follow his example.

**Preparation**

Everyone should read Days 26–32.
Set up chairs and facilities as usual.

**Getting started**

Open with prayer and/or singing, as appropriate.
Introduce any new members.
Ask participants to talk in twos and threes about the first job they ever dreamed of having. (It doesn't matter if they ever got that job—it's the dreaming that matters.) Ask them to explain to each other why they found this particular job attractive.

**Getting involved**

Share that information with the larger group. But have the information come from the listener in each group of two or three.
Try to list these responses on a flipchart in two groups:
• jobs desired because of what they could do for the person
• jobs desired because of what the person could do for others.
But don't identify the two groups of jobs until all the ideas have been presented, to avoid influencing the way people describe their reasons for wanting a particular job.
Since they're probably about adolescent aspirations, many of these "dream" jobs may have self-serving motives. If so, point out that emphasis. If not, congratulate the group on their selfless idealism!

**Starting the thoughts**

Note that in listening, people were actually serving each other. (If anyone couldn't describe another person's dreamed occupation, because they either failed to listen closely enough or did too much talking, their embarrassment should make this point quite evident.)
Comment, as necessary, about the general lack of popularity, in our culture, of service occupations. Few people *want* to be bus drivers, housemaids, waiters, hospital interns, etc. Compare that with a similar attitude in Jesus' time, when the ideal was to be an owner, an employer, a host—rather than a tenant, a servant, a recipient of charity.
Present the ideals of service of humility that Jesus' modelled for his disciples, based on the reading for Day 26, the 4th Sunday of Lent. (Don't bother dealing with the differences between John's gospel and

the other three gospels, unless you particularly want to.)

(As usual, you may simply play the cassette tape instead of making a presentation, if you prefer.)

### Grounding thoughts in scripture

Read in unison Isaiah 53:1–3, and Philippians 2:5-11.

You could read John 13:3–15 in unison. But it will probably have greater impact if you have a dramatized reading, with one person reading the part of Jesus, another Peter, and a third narrating.

Have them read it again, this time with more life and vigor in their words. People should be able to hear Jesus' exasperation, Peter's frustration, etc.

If necessary, do it a third time, with even more expression! By the end, people should have a clear impression—in their hearts as well as their heads—of the shock of Jesus taking the humble role of a despised and ignored servant.

### Applying new understandings to life

Divide into smaller groups for discussion, depending on the original size of your study group. Discuss the following questions as time permits (or create your own questions).

1. To parents, *How often do you feel like your children's servants?* And to children (of any age), *How often do you feel like servants to your parents?* Remember that feelings cannot be challenged; if people feel like a servant, that is truth for them.
2. *What are the benefits or personal rewards of humble service?* Try to have people give personal examples, if possible.
3. *How would you try to sell that idea to others?* Suppose the group were launching an advertising campaign for servant roles....

### Putting it together

If you have divided into several groups for discussion, gather together again.

Invite participants to volunteer insights they may have gained during the discussion. Particularly encourage insights related to current situations that people face, rather than intellectual understandings.

Avoid, if possible, a reporting by a leader of what groups discussed.

### Closing

End with prayer, music if appropriate, and a blessing or benediction.

**Day 33**                         *Fifth Sunday of Lent*

# *Remembrance of me*

According to legend, when Dr. Peter Bryce was minister of Metropolitan United Church in downtown Toronto, he put everyone onto a committee of some kind. If there were no committees to put a newcomer into, Dr Bryce would create a new committee especially for that person! He would not tolerate *anyone* being uninvolved.

He knew that people don't become committed to a cause because they have studied it. Not even because they consider it worthwhile. They only commit themselves when they're involved. Peace movements, political parties, relief agencies, even social organizations— all recognize at least subconsciously this principle, and do their best to get people *actively* involved.

I once wrote an article about workers on a politician's election campaign. I expected that those workers, knowing politics from the inside, would be much more cynical about the political process than Canadians in general. To my surprise, the more deeply these campaign workers got involved, the more passionately they believed in what they were doing. Even when trying to sabotage a competitor's campaign, they believed totally in the rightness of their cause.

Modern adult education theory stresses some element of action in any teaching program. People learn not just with their minds, but also with their bodies; they integrate the information presented to them by doing something with it. The sermon, where people simply sit passively while someone preaches at them, may be the worst educational vehicle ever invented!

Jesus would not have known about these education theories. But he clearly recognized the principle. *"Do* this..." he said in celebrating the Last Supper (Luke 22:17–20; I Corinthians 11:23–25).

It was by far the most successful of all his enacted parables. It had to be. It was, quite literally, his last chance. For immediately after that supper (if we ignore the lengthy speeches in John's gospel), he and his followers went out into the streets of Jerusalem. And a few hours later, he was arrested.

He had, therefore, no way of testing to see if his enacted parable had taken hold. That test did not come until the day after the resurrection, when two disciples were walking from Jerusalem to the village of Emmaus, (Luke 24:13–31). Along the way, they encountered a stranger. They told him the rumors of the resurrection sweeping through Jerusalem that day; the stranger then used two hours or so while they walked to show them how this remarkable event fulfilled the scriptures.

Wanting to hear more, the two invited the stranger to join them for supper. But they still didn't recognize him. Until he broke the bread, and passed it to them....

In that *doing*, they recognized something they hadn't seen in a face, or heard in a voice, or even perceived in a message.

That action has also proved the most durable of his enacted parables. Not all Christian denominations wash feet, or attack religious commercialism, or practise humility—though Jesus clearly advocated all these actions. But nearly all denominations have some form of the Last Supper as a central sacrament. And they continue to enact—to act out—that sacrament. The words alone do not suffice—the bread *must be broken*, the cup *must be poured*.

Two factors, I suspect, made this enacted parable more successful than others.

First, it made the disciples active participants.

That's a subtle but significant distinction. All of the other enacted parables involved them only indirectly.

During the triumphal entry, one or more of the disciples may have hung back, thinking, perhaps: "In a city where people tried to stone you not that long ago, this is a pretty dumb way to avoid drawing attention to yourself!"

No doubt in the Temple, several disciples cowered in a corner, hoping they could get away before the guards arrived.

At Bethany, they were bystanders, observing while the woman anointed Jesus with ointment.

Even while he washed their feet, they didn't have to *do* anything in return. They could just sit.

But when the person next to you plunks a piece of broken bread in your palm, you have to *do* something with it. At the very least, you have to pass it on. You can't just leave it sitting there. You have to take some of it, breaking that bread/body again with your own hands. Or else you have to decide *not* to take any.

The breaking and passing of bread offers no middle ground, no way to avoid involvement. The same holds true for the cup.

Secondly, in choosing the dual symbols of bread and wine, Jesus drew together a vast and powerful range of memories.

And though the disciples didn't know it at the time, the bread and wine would also tie that supper together inextricably with the traumatic events of the coming days.

"I will not eat this bread again," Jesus told them, and "I will not drink the fruit of the vine again." The words confirmed what they all knew, instinctively—their time together was rushing towards an end.

As at any imminent farewell, their thoughts might

drift back over the many meals they had shared together. Corn, gathered fresh in the fields. Feasts and parties that offended John the Baptist's more straight-laced disciples. Banquets with upper-crust Pharisees, and crusts with beggars.

The bread that Jesus held in his hands might remind them of some of his statements. "I am the bread of life," he said, according to John's recollections. "The bread of God... comes from heaven and gives life to the world.... Anyone who feeds on this bread will live forever." (John 6:25–59).

They would recall other occasions when he had taken bread in his hands, and broken it. All four gospels describe one episode, when some 5,000 men—and an unknown number of women and children—followed him beside the lake in Galilee (Matthew 14:13–21; Mark 6:30–34; Luke 9:10–17; John 6:1–13). Matthew and Mark also refer to a second feeding, of 4,000 (Matthew 15:32–39; Mark 8:1–10). Jesus took the bread available—five loaves with two fishes one time, seven loaves and "a few fish" the second—blessed them, broke them, and passed them out.

At Passover time—the event they had come to Jerusalem to celebrate—they would naturally also think of the central story of their people, the exodus from Egypt. The bread that Jesus broke represented the unleavened bread baked by the Israelites to take with them in their flight into the desert.

The wine might remind them of what John describes as Jesus' first miracle, making wine from water at the wedding reception in Cana (John 2:1–11). Or of his conversation with the Samaritan woman at the well (John 4:4–30). He had talked with her of "living water"—"Whoever drinks the drink that I give will never suffer thirst any more..."

Dark in the lamplight, the wine would have looked

like blood. Jesus drew attention to that similarity: "This is my blood of the covenant, poured out for you."

His reference to blood of the covenant would also recall their traditions. Blood, in Jewish medicine and mythology, was one of the two signs of life. (The other was breath.) When the priests made sacrifices, they splashed the blood of their sacrifices—literally the blood of life—against the altar. In doing so, they maintained a practice that went back to Moses in the desert. To mark the covenant between God and Israel, Moses threw some of the blood against the altar; he threw the rest over the people (Exodus 24:6-8). That blood, in turn, represented the blood of the animals the Hebrew people ate the night before leaving Egypt. They painted that blood on their doorposts and lintels, so that the Angel of Death would "pass over" their homes, and save their firstborn sons from death (Exodus 12:7, 12-13).

Ironically, *this* blood would not save *this* firstborn son.

The little group may even have been dimly aware that in sharing bread and drink, they shared the universal needs of all humans. Especially poor humans. Affluent people can afford the luxury of differences. An abundance of fish and game and housing materials gave the native nations of the Pacific coast free time to develop their unique artistry. Affluence—relatively speaking—allowed our ancestors to launch the industrial revolution; it enables us to measure our status by how many cars we own, or how many bathrooms we have in our homes. It lets us pamper ourselves with white bread that tastes and feels like sponge rubber.

But poverty is pretty much the same, the world over. And unleavened bread is the food of poverty. Even the names, incredibly, are often similar. A disk of *pita* in the Middle East looks and tastes much like a *chapati* in India; with some cheese and tomato paste added, it becomes a *pizza* in Italy....

Sharing unleavened bread, even ceremonially, the disciples were no longer doing something for "the poor," but for a moment shared their lives.

In our practice of the Last Supper, we have lost that sense of unity with the poor and the oppressed. Some of our churches use individual wafers, pressed flat as rice paper, as uniform as an industrial society can make them. Other churches use antiseptic cubes of a leavened loaf, its bleached whiteness a sign of flaunted affluence. Only a few use darker flour, with a bit of bran left in it, or a loaf that must be torn and broken by each participant. But even that loaf is always baked with yeast, and often sweeter than normal bread.

We diverge, too, in our *reasons* for sharing in the supper.

I come from a Reformed Church heritage, on the Presbyterian side, which emphasized the Eucharist as a *Last* Supper. It treated Communion mainly as a memorial, a special occasion. Special occasions must not happen too often, lest they become commonplace. On the other hand, during the 1970s when the United and Anglican Churches of Canada were negotiating towards church union, I interviewed a number of Anglican ministers. From them, I learned that Anglicans see the Eucharist primarily as a *Supper*, a meal to nurture the spirit, and therefore to be taken as often as needed.

Looking back, I think both traditions missed the point of what Jesus was trying to teach. His Last Supper was more than a meal, and more than a memorial. He wanted his followers to remember *him*—all that he was, all that he did and said, all that he stood for. And to remember that they were part of that.

By brilliant planning, by sudden inspiration, or by

sheer good luck, Jesus summarized his life and his teaching in a single simple act. It was so simple, it happened every day. It bound them into solidarity with the poor people Jesus had loved and championed, into solidarity with their own history, into solidarity with their own life experience.

Whenever they broke bread again, they would once again share his life. Sharing his life—his blood, the symbol of life. And sharing his cause—a commitment so strong not even the breaking of his body could deflect him.

In remembrance of him, we become him.

### Reading: Luke 22:17-20
### The Last Supper

*When you celebrate with a special meal,
with whom do you express your solidarity?
Do your table settings, your choice of foods,
emulate the lifestyles of the wealthy?
How often have you deliberately eaten like the poor?*

**Day 34** *Monday*

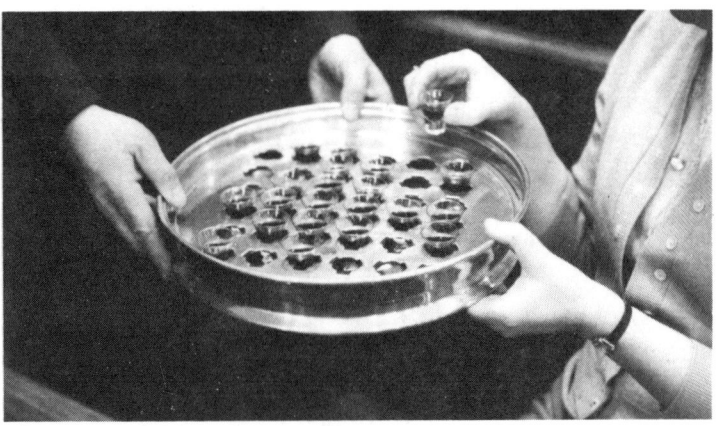

By chance, I attended three different celebrations of the Last Supper within a week. All three services used similar words; all three followed a similar liturgy; all three used grape juice and torn bread.

But what those three churches did with that bread and juice suggested some surprising differences in their understanding of the sacrament.

The first two churches distributed the bread and juice to members sitting in the pews. One did it with well-rehearsed military precision, the other with folksy casualness. But the differences went much deeper than that.

In the first service, worshippers ate their bread and drank their juice as soon as they received it. Then they passed the bread or juice along to their neighbors, murmuring, "Jesus Christ, the bread of life," or "Jesus Christ, the true vine."

In the second, everyone waited until all had received; then everyone ate or drank simultaneously. They passed the bread or juice in silence.

At the third service, people shuffled up the aisle to receive a piece of bread at the front, to dip it in a cup, to swallow it, and then to get out of the way.

The actions of the first service, it seems to me, made Communion a personal matter. Eating and drinking alone emphasized each individual's private relationship with God. The words—even if only murmured—implied the individual's connection to one's neighbor, a sense of serving others.

The actions of the second service emphasized community. No one ate, until all ate together. It suggested an equality, a sharing out of common property. But nothing in it implied responsibility, or commitment to a larger task.

The people lining up in the third service reminded me of a breadline. Clearly, the worship leaders owned the bread and the wine; they controlled how much each person received, and dispensed the blessing. The lay people simply received; they neither served each other nor shared in a communal act.

None of those three churches would *say* that was their theology; probably few of the people would even *think* it. But that's what they *acted out*.

### Reading: James 1:22–25
### Doers of the word

*Why do some crowds line up calmly
at cashiers and ticket wickets,
while others push and shove?
Why do some people resort to violence to solve problems?
Are they acting out their unexamined beliefs,
their hidden theology?
How do your actions reflect your beliefs?*

**Day 35**                                           *Tuesday*

Eating alone is lonely. Few people eat alone, if they can help it.

One night I sat alone in a crowded restaurant in Ottawa, eating Chinese food. In the whole restaurant, only two others sat by themselves. One of them hid herself behind her newspaper; the other buried his face in a novel.

Everyone else sat in twos, or threes, or more.

At the end of the meal, the waitress brought me the bill, with a candy and a fortune cookie.

As I broke the cookie open, to see what the little slip of paper inside would say, suddenly memories flooded in on me of many other meals involving fortune cookies. Driving to a Chinese restaurant with a group of university students after university dances, for late snacks. Arriving at the re-created gold rush town of Barkerville one evening with my family, and finding only the Chinese restaurant open after dark. Taking visiting relatives from Ireland to a feast in Chinatown, watching them go goggle-eyed at the strangeness of the experience.

Each time, we laughed at the silly fortunes we read in our fortune cookies.

But I realize now, the good fortune wasn't in the cookie at all. We ourselves were silly, expecting to discover good news in a slip of paper. The real fortune was in the company we shared.

**Reading: Matthew 18:19–20
Where two or three are gathered**

*Think back over some of the really good times of your life.
What were you doing?
Did the doing make it a good time?
Or the company you did it with?*

**Day 36**  Wednesday

I had been away from home and family for about six weeks, on a writing and editing assignment in Africa. As usual on such trips, I worked seven days a week, researching, writing, preparing materials for the printer....

One morning in Blantyre, Malawi, with the September sun slanting through the purple blossoms of the jacaranda tree outside my window, I heard singing. It sounded like a hymn, though the music had a robust flavor I was not accustomed to in Canadian churches. I realized I hadn't been to church for several weeks.

The sounds led me to the Presbyterian church. A number of black people looked in through the windows; a crowd of them stood outside the doors. I wasn't sure I could get in, but they parted to let me through.

The church was filled. Blacks, and a few whites, jammed together in the pews. Some wore polished shoes; some had no shoes at all. An elderly man, black scalp gleaming through pure white hair, squeezed over to make room for me. He found me the place in the hymnbook.

I couldn't read a word of it. The whole service was in Chichewa, the local dialect. I understand none of the hymns, none of the preaching.

Until the end of the service, that is. But when the minister stood, and raised the bread, and broke it, I knew exactly what he was saying: "This bread is my body, broken for you."

And when he held up the cup, I knew again what he was saying: "This cup is the new covenant in my blood. Drink it in remembrance of me."

The *words* were different.

The *Word* was the same.

Until then, I had been feeling lost, a stranger in an alien land. Suddenly, I realized that although I was halfway around the world from my home, I was at home. I was among fellow Christians. I was part of a universal family.

### Reading: Luke 24:13–32
### Recognized by his actions

*Have you ever forgotten someone's name,*
*even the person's face,*
*but suddenly recognized a gesture of the hand,*
*a toss of the head?*
*The disciples didn't expect to see Jesus again.*
*Was that what broke the blindness of their grief?*

Excerpted from An Everyday God, pp. 16–17.

# Day 37                              *Thursday*

Sometimes ordinary little things have more impact than the big things.

The last night of Stephen's life, he no longer had enough strength to hold up his head. In a pale green hospital room, with a night-light glowing on the wall, we held his head up for him, to keep his throat straight, to give him every possible chance for each breath.

He tried to cough one last time. And stopped breathing.

As we lowered his body gently back onto his pillows. I glanced at his bedside radio, still muttering the murky lyrics of his favorite rock station. A pale orange light illuminated the digits of the clock. It said 11:17.

The months passed, and we almost got used to not having him around the house. We no longer listened for his familiar "Hello 'ello?" as he came in the back door. We settled his life insurance, and gave away his clothes. We told ourselves we were coping with our grief.

But every time I looked at a clock, as we headed off to bed, it said 11:17. I never got used to it.

Every time, it took me back to a pale green hospital room, with a night-light glowing on the wall, and a son taking his last breath.

### Reading: 2 Samuel 18:33
### A father's grief

*Everyone has lost someone.*
*A parent, a friend who moved away forever.*
*What do you remember most clearly about them?*
*Special events, fine statements? Or little daily habits?*
*Why do we pay so little attention*
*to the little daily things in our own lives?*

**Day 38**                                      *Friday*

One winter night, I had to drive 150 kilometres in a blizzard.

Usually, at night, you can see *something* along the highway—street lights in the distance; gravel by the side of the road; trees blacker even than the sky. In that blizzard, no street lights winked comfortingly; no towns to the side gave a sense of perspective. My headlights bored a flickering tunnel of white straight ahead. Ribbons of white whirled toward me like tracer bullets.

I had no idea where the road was. The snow hid any trace of contours, of color, of textur, between the highway and the shoulder of the road, and the invisible fields beyond that. I had only one way of knowing that I was still on the road—ahead of me, I could see the tail lights of a semi-trailer.

I suppose he was following someone's tail lights ahead of him.

In the same way, someone else stayed on the road by following me.

So we raced through the night. It felt like racing—I have no idea how fast we actually drove, for I never dared take my eyes off the road to check my speedometer. A chain of vehicles, following each other, desperately hoping that none of us ever lost the way.

In our faith, too, we follow each other, often blindly. In the beginning, the Christian church was known as "The Way." Its members didn't know where they were going any better than I did, in that blizzard. They knew only what those who had gone before them had done, and those before them, and those before them…

The disciples probably celebrated the Lord's Supper partly because Jesus had—and partly because they didn't know what else to do. So they passed the tradition on. Right down to us.

We can see no further ahead in life than in a

blizzard. And time won't slow down to let us figure things out. So each generation hurtles headlong into the problems of its own time, unable to do more—most of the time—than trust that those who went before knew where to find the road.

Maybe that's what faith is—trusting those who went before, and those who will come after. And passing on what others need, to follow us.

### Reading: 1 Corinthians 11:23-28
### Passing the tradition along

*How many daily rituals do you observe?*
*From dropping the ticket in the bus box in the morning,*
*to shaking the newspaper straight in the evening?*
*Do all repeated actions become rituals?*
*Does the Lord's Supper become just a ritual,*
*a commonplace action of no significance?*

*Remembrance of me*

### Day 39 — Saturday

One summer, towards the end of my university years, I worked as a temporary customs officer in Kingsgate, on the Canada/US border. Kingsgate was, and still is, a very small place—a highway, a railway, a river, and a scattering of houses along the valley. Eastport, on the south side of the border, was fractionally larger—it also had a hotel.

The whole community had only one space available for rent to students—a lean-to apartment more or less attached to the side of the hotel. I never knew for sure whether the hotel held up the apartment, or the apartment held up the hotel.

The apartment had one large room. Two of us needed accommodation. So Ron MacKenzie and I agreed to share it.

Inevitably, over four months in fairly close quarters, friction developed. Ron liked his porridge thin and his pancakes thick; I liked mine the exact opposite. Ron put pepper in his salads; I put pepper in the scrambled eggs. Ron liked pasta; I liked potatoes.

One day these petty irritations flared over an even more petty matter. We both smoked pipes back then—more for appearance than for pleasure, I admit. Ron had bought a big can of tobacco, and told me to help myself. I bought some of my own—a different brand. Ron felt slighted. We ended up shouting at each other, nose to nose, like a confrontation in an old-fashioned western movie.

Fortunately for the rest of the summer, we talked the conflict out. Like a scene from that old western movie, we shook hands. "Let's go into the hotel and have a drink together," Ron said, to seal the deal.

Funny, isn't it, how having a drink together symbolizes harmony. You can't drink with someone while holding a grudge. Conversely, in the old westerns, if you refused a drink, you risked insulting the giver. In our culture—perhaps in all cultures—the act of sharing another's hospitality, of having a drink together, whether it's tea or tequila, bonds people into friendship.

Maybe it has something to do with our universal need for water.

Whatever it was, Jesus raised it to a whole new level of meaning it when he raised the cup, and said, "In this cup, you see a new covenant..."

### Reading: John 4:5–14
### The living water

*Think about your acquaintances and your close friends.
What's the difference between them?
Do you take time to eat and drink with acquaintances?
Or do you save that privilege for friends?*

## Session Five

### Purpose
This session tries to help people realize why the Last Supper has been such a powerful ritual in the Christian Church for close to 20 centuries.

### Preparation
All participants should have read Day 33–39 in the book.

Set up chairs and other facilities needed as usual.

Draw, or find an artist in the group who can draw for you, a very large vine on the floor or on a roll of brown wrapping paper. The main stem of the vine should be about the middle, with tendrils, leaves, and bunches of grapes extending well out to both ends. The vine should be long enough for everyone in the group to stand on it!

### Getting started
Open with prayer and/or singing, as usual.

Welcome any newcomers, and make sure they are introduced to the regulars, and vice versa.

Read John 15:1–4. Ask people to reflect in silence, for a minute or so, what kind of branch they might be, on that vine.

Then have them get up, and stand on whatever part of the drawn vine they feel most closely represents their typical role in the church. They may choose to be near the main stem, or way out at an end. They may feel like the fruit, or like leaves, or even like a bare branch.

### Getting involved
Ask each person to explain briefly why he or she chose that particular place to stand. The explanations may be as surprising as the location. For example, one person may be out at an end, because he feels cut off from much of the church; another may be out at the end because she feels that's where the plant is growing.

Remember that—as in brainstorming—anyone may ask questions of the person speaking, for clarification. But no one may challenge or argue with anyone else's explanation.

Ask if anyone was surprised at where they chose to stand (or ended up standing), or at the reasons that they had for choosing that location on the vine.

### Starting the thoughts
Inform the group that they have just put into practice a current principle of adult education—that we learn with our bodies and our actions, as well as with our minds. (Some may have found that their

bodies told them something about their relationship to the church that differed from what their minds had told them during the period of silent reflection.)

Develop some of the ideas in the reading for Day 33, the 5th Sunday of Lent. Emphasize particularly the physical involvement of the disciples in breaking the bread and passing the wine.

If possible, find some headlines in this week's newspapers which deal with famine or poverty somewhere in the world. Use those headlines to make a continuing connection between the poverty meal of the Israelites fleeing into the desert and the starvation diet of people today, with the Last Supper.

(Or, if you prefer, simply play the casette tape.)

### Grounding thoughts in scripture

Have the participants follow a sequence of readings through the Old Testament into the life of the early church. (To provide more active involvement, read all passages aloud, together.)
- Genesis 4:1–10, Abel's blood cries out to God from the soil
- Exodus 12:3–14, the blood of sacrifice on doorposts, so the Lord would "pass over."
- Exodus 24:3–8, the blood marking a covenant between God and the people.
- Jeremiah 31:31–33, the coming of a new covenant.
- Luke 22:14–20, the Last Supper.
- 1 Corinthians 11:20–29, the meaning of the sacrament.

Invite any comments that people may want to make, or any insights they may wish to share, as a result of reading this series of passages.

### Applying new understandings to life

Divide into smaller groups, if appropriate. Use the following questions to stimulate discussion, or create your own questions, based on the readings from Days 34–39.

1. *When you invite quests to your home, do you put out your best silver and china?* Almost everyone will say yes, of course. Prod to find out why they use it for guests, and not for everyday family. Are guests more valuable than family? Do they want to impress the guests, but not their friends? What kind of lifestyle are they pretending to live? Ask a lot of *Why* questions.... (You may need to reassure participants that these questions are not intended to judge their lifestyle, but only to explore assumptions they may not have considered before.)

2. *Have you ever experienced real poverty or hunger? When, and where?* Encourage personal stories. Draw attention to ways in which

these stories may express common themes, even though they may be quite different superficially. (Remember that poverty is not limited to the Depression of the '30s, nor to underdeveloped countries. University students, wartime refugees, native people, even tourists who have lost their credit cards, may all have experienced poverty and hunger—if only temporarily.)

3. *Are there any good things about poverty and hunger?* Some may say no; others may talk about willingness to share, sense of community, how good simple food tasted, etc.

### Putting it together

If you divided into several groups for discussion, gather together again.

Invite participants to volunteer insights they may have gained during the discussion. In this session, some experiences that people have had—possibly in wartime, or as volunteers in work overseas, in downtown missions, in remote communities—may be so moving and compelling that the larger group should hear them.

### Closing

End with prayer, music if appropriate, and a blessing or benediction.

**Day 40**  *Palm Sunday*

# Waiting for the end

In a state of shock, any kind of shock, people no longer react normally. In wartime, for example, soldiers may perform incredible feats of bravery. They carry wounded comrades to safety through a hail of bullets. They scale cliffs, slog across swamps, and storm impregnable gun emplacements.

In civilian life, people badly wounded in accidents may feel no pain. People shattered by grief may act quite normally, almost hyper-rationally.

All of these reactions result from shock.

At an early stage of shock, major and minor crises blend. Capturing a cannon seems no more or less difficult than pouring a glass of orange juice. Some will do either, with equal indifference. Others can do neither; they freeze into immobility.

At a later stage of shock, reactions reverse. Big problems become small; small ones seem overwhelming. A broken shoelace defeats a soldier who has just won a Victoria Cross; the survivor of a car accident worries more about a missed appointment than a demolished vehicle.

Reading the accounts of Jesus' arrest and trial, I have sometimes wondered if he was also in shock. Does that account for his calmness, his silence under questioning, his courage when faced with certain death?

It's possible. No human can withstand a sustained interrogation, physical beating, and a night's lack of sleep without some effects. But I don't think that shock controlled Jesus' behavior.

I reach that conclusion because of his actions in the Garden of Gethsemane.

Usually, when we read the story of his prayers under the olive trees, we concentrate on his grief, or on the lack of support he received from his friends. We don't ask an obvious question—*why did he wait so long?*

He and his friends had been staying in Bethany, outside Jerusalem, to keep clear of danger. That danger came, not from the Roman governor, but from the Temple authorities. Roman soldiers had no fear of civilian crowds. If the Romans wanted to arrest Jesus, they would have done so without hesitation, crowds or no crowds.

The Temple had guards. But since the Romans would not tolerate a competitive force of trained troops, the Temple guards could never be more than a local police force, keeping law and order. They would correspond, I suppose, to bouncers at a night club—rough, tough, but hardly ready to put down riots.

The Temple authorities had plenty of opportunities to arrest him in Jerusalem. He was, Luke's gospel tells us, "teaching in the Temple every day" (Luke 21:37). But they didn't arrest him. Clearly, they weren't willing to risk arresting Jesus when other people were around. So Jesus was relatively safe in Jerusalem during the day.

Presumably, he was also relatively safe in the much smaller village of Bethany at night, as long as he had lots of company around.

The route Jesus and his disciples took from Jerusalem to Bethany might go *over* the Mount of Olives, or it might go *around*, as the modern highway does. Either way, the Garden of Gethsemane was more or less on the way. During the Passover period, the main route would probably have a number of people on it, day or night. But the garden was private property. Only the owner's friends could enter.

Jesus obviously had a habit of stopping in that

garden for some peace and quiet. But why did he stay so long this night?

The disciples certainly didn't expect him to stay so long. Most of them fell asleep, waiting.

He wasn't content with just one period of private prayer. Three times, he left his disciples to nod in the moonlight while he went off by himself (Matthew 26:36–46; Mark 14:32–42). Why not simply continue on to Bethany and safety?

Why wait, in fact, in *the one place where he could safely be arrested?*

I can come to only one conclusion. Jesus waited there *because* it was the one place where he could safely be arrested.

I don't imply that he engineered the event. Nor do I suggest that Judas simply carried out Jesus' instructions by betraying him to the high priests—though both those ideas could be argued.

I simply contend that Jesus knew two things:
1. If he was going to be arrested, it would have to be an out-of-the-way place, not in a community or on a main route.
2. Gethsemane fitted the requirements, and was a place he was known to go.

So he waited....

No wonder it was such an agonizing wait. No wonder he sweated it out under the olive trees.

Because the authorities almost bungled the arrest. Their raggle-taggle band of bouncers were late getting there—so late that if he had given up and left after two extended periods of prayer, they'd have missed him.

That premise—that Jesus deliberately delayed in Gethsemane so that he could be arrested—throws the trial into a different light. If you accept the premise, you can no longer assume that his behavior during the trial

*Waiting for the end*

resulted from shock. Rather, you have to ask what Jesus expected that his trial would accomplish. Or, in line with the rest of this book, what lesson he wanted to teach his followers.

We can only guess. For from the moment of his arrest, he lost any opportunity to explain his actions. On other occasions, his disciples could take him aside and ask questions. "What did you mean?" they asked of his parables. Or, after his healings, "How could you do that, and we couldn't?"

But much of the trial has to have come to us through hearsay. Some of the events may have been told, later, by priests who converted to the new Christian faith, or by servants who gossiped. But neither priests nor servants would have attempted, or even have thought of, asking him to explain his behavior during the trial.

So we have to guess.

We can assume that he was in shock.

We can argue that he was actually in control—even though the evidence suggests otherwise. (I suspect that such arguments tell us more about the arguers' own convictions that the Messiah must be a conquering hero than about Jesus himself.)

We can see him as a helpless victim. That's an increasingly popular interpretation. It recognizes his humanity. It links Jesus' experience with the trials of many other humans.

But I believe that none of those adequately describes his behavior. He was not simply calm, or submissive, or resigned. He was certainly not afraid. As I read the stories of the trial, the word that best describes him seems to be *confident*.

I think that Jesus was acting out a real-life parable. He had tried to tell it in words, and his disciples kept missing the point. As long as he was with them, conventional concepts of leadership kept blinding them to both his words and his actions. By acting out his message, Jesus forced them to put two and two together.

John, at least, seems to have gotten that message—though possibly years later. So John tells us that Jesus said to Pilate: "My kingdom is not of this world...." (It might make more sense slightly paraphrased: "My kingdom is not like those of this world. If it were, my followers would have used force....") Three times in that brief exchange of words, John has Jesus refer to himself as a king (John 18:33–38).

And that is out of character for Jesus. Usually, he avoided identification as a ruler of any kind. In Galilee, when people awed by Jesus' miracles wanted to "make him king by force," says John, "he slipped away into the hills by himself" (John 6:15).

What was the parable that Jesus acted? If he had used words, it might have gone something like this:

"Once there was a sovereign, whose realm was organized to be totally just, totally fair to everyone. The ruler was confident that all was in order, but just to make sure, he decided to test it. So he disguised himself as a poor person, one who had no position or status to protect him.

"He went out into the country. As might be expected, he got into trouble, and was wrongly arrested.

"He was brought to trial. But he was confident that he would ultimately receive justice. He had so much confidence in that ultimate justice that he refused to reveal his true identity. He wouldn't defend himself against false charges. Not when he was beaten, not when he was sentenced, not even when he was being executed, did he stop believing that in the end justice would be done."

The parable remains unfinished; we have to supply the ending.

If the parable he acted out simply ends on the cross, we would have to conclude that his confidence was misplaced. He did not receive the justice he expected. He was wrongly, unfairly executed as a common criminal.

But if we believe that his enacted parable ends not on Good Friday but on Easter morning, then he was blindingly, blazingly, right.

### Reading: Mark 14:53–72, 15:1–5; John 18:33–38
### On trial

*How often do you feel like saying, "I told you so"?*
*(Do you bite your tongue to keep from saying it more often?)*
*When someone admits you were right,*
*does it make the pain of the disagreement worth while?*
*Do you think Jesus might be saying,*
*"I told you so,"*
*to us?*

See also *Two Worlds in One,* pp117–118

**Day 41**                                                      *Monday*

I hate waiting. I particularly hate waiting helplessly.

One time, Joan asked me to meet her at the airport. I left in plenty of time to reach the airport before her arrival—if a tractor-trailer loaded with lumber hadn't dumped its load all over Highway 401. Traffic crawled like a poorly co-ordinated centipede.

Normally, driving to the airport takes 30 minutes. This time, it took 90.

When I finally got there, I was so late that Joan's flight arrival information had been removed from the information displays. She had already been waiting an hour. But I couldn't find her.

I searched for her all over the airport, for over an hour... Finally I gave up, and drove home.

Traffic hadn't improved. It took another 90 minutes. But when I got there, she was waiting for me. She must have come out one door at the airport to catch a cab, as I went in another door. She had been delayed just as long in traffic as I had.

She doesn't like waiting either.

We did not have a pleasant homecoming.

And yet we had both looked forward to that homecoming. If waiting for a welcome event can be so unpleasant, I wonder how Jesus must have felt, waiting for something that he knew would be extremely unpleasant....

### Reading: Mark 14:32–42
### Waiting for the arrest

*How do you pass the time,*
*when waiting for a train, a bus, a plane, an appointment?*
*Do you read, pace, fuss, fume?*
*Do you pray?*

*Waiting for the end*

# Day 42 — Tuesday

Several years ago, I read a book on theology which spent an extraordinary amount of effort showing that the words we usually read as "betrayed" really meant "handed over" in the original Greek.

I didn't get the point then. I do now. Because recently, I "handed over" our cat Tuppence to the vet.

Tuppence was more than 19 years old, stone deaf, nearly blind, and almost toothless. But she was still alive, still part of our family.

Then one morning, her left cheek puffed out as if she had a marble tucked into it. The veterinarian, a kindly woman who genuinely loves animals, examined Tuppence. One of Tuppence's remaining teeth had abscessed.

Carefully, the veterinarian explained our alternatives. "We can remove the tooth surgically, but at her age—" she shrugged.

"She might die?" I asked.

She nodded. "We have to give a general anesthetic. It will leave her disoriented, probably unable to drink or eat for several days. In her weakened state—"

"She might die?" I asked.

She nodded. "We could try to treat it with antibiotics, but—"

"She might die anyway?"

She nodded. "She hasn't the strength to withstand the infection without it. We could leave it alone—"

"And she'll die," I finished flatly.

She nodded.

All our choices narrowed to the same result. Tuppence would die without surgery. She'd probably die during surgery. Even if she survived surgery, its effects would seriously shorten her life.

I picked Tuppence up one last time, and stroked her head. She purred. It broke my heart. She lay in my

arms, and she purred.

"Would you like to be with her?" the vet asked.

I didn't know what to say. "I'd recommend not," the vet went on. "We give her a tranquilizer so she's relatively calm. But it's still not pleasant—"

With a sick feeling, I handed Tuppence over to her.

In that moment, I understood the theologian's point. For Tuppence, being "handed over"—even to the kindest and most gentle of veterinarians—was the end. And we all knew it.

For Jesus, being "handed over" to the local authorities—who were anything but kind and gentle—was also the end. And everyone knew it.

The familiar words in Mark's gospel—"The hour has come! The Son of Man is betrayed into the hands of sinners"—fail to convey the finality of being "handed over."

**Reading: Acts 26:30–27:1
Handed over**

*Have you ever given up hope?
But you're still here.
Where, and how, did you find the hope to continue?*

# Day 43 — Wednesday

The Czechoslovakian immigration official stood at the door of the bus.

"TAY-LOR!" he barked.

I stepped forward. The official peered closely at me, comparing my face with the photo in my passport.

Then he nodded, and looked at the name on the next passport. "SCOTT!"

It was a strange feeling, being completely in someone else's power. If that immigration official decided that one of us was not the person we claimed to be—the person to whom the passport belonged—we wouldn't be allowed into his country. No protests of innocence, character witnesses, or evidence to the contrary could change his verdict.

Jesus must have felt like that, standing on trial before chief priests and elders.

They were in charge. They controlled the court. They had the guards. Jesus was their prisoner. And he had no way of defending himself. By his own words, he condemned himself. He might as well have pleaded guilty.

Under the laws of that time and place, it was an open-and-shut case. Except that in the strange way that history has, it's no longer Jesus who is on trial, but the chief priests and their aides.

### Reading: Colossians 2:12–15
### Turning the tables

*When you watch a movie, do you cheer*
*when the victim, against all odds,*
*turns the tables on the bad guys?*
*Is that how the early church saw the Resurrection?*

**Day 44** *Thursday*

A friend's world fell apart, a few years ago. Everything that she had once taken for granted, she now found herself questioning.

For the first time in her life, she read the Bible from beginning to end. And she was shocked.

"How can you worship that God?" she demanded. "For every occasion when God is loving and compassionate, there are five times when that same God is vicious, vindictive, and cruel!" She documented charge after charge, incident after incident where God destroyed people, cities, nations, even whole tribes of Israel itself, utterly, totally, without a shred of mercy.

"But that's the Old Testament," I countered weakly. "Maybe their understanding of God was still growing."

"It's no better in the New Testament," she retorted. "As a person, Jesus is wonderful. But the fulcrum of the New Testament—the point on which everything else hinges—is the Crucifixion. What kind of God would orchestrate such cruelty? What kind of God would allow an innocent man to die so hideously? What kind of God would stand by and allow such a miscarriage of justice?"

I tried to interrupt, but her challenges poured on: "Would you do that to *your* son? What would you think of a father who did?"

Not much, I must admit. When I hear of brutal parents beating or even killing their children, I get very angry. Could a criminal act for humans be considered a virtue for God?

I grasped for a doctrinal straw. "You're assuming that God was somewhere off in heaven watching all this," I said to her. "But what if that was *God* on that cross?"

She stopped in mid-flight, trying to absorb the implications of that idea.

"Isn't that," I plunged on, "what the doctrine of

*Waiting for the end*

Incarnation is about? That whoever or whatever God is, God became one of us? A way of saying that God would never inflict on us anything that God wasn't willing to share..."

I ran out of words.

"If that's true," she said slowly, "it *does* make a difference."

### Reading: Philippians 2:5–8
### Even to death

*When things go wrong, do you get angry?*
*Do you blame yourself? Or others?*
*Do you blame God for causing your suffering?*
*Would it make any difference*
*if you felt that God was suffering with you?*

**Day 45**  *Good Friday*

# *The cross*

When Jesus allowed himself to be arrested, instead of proceeding to the relative safety of Bethany, he gave up any direct control over what would happen to him. His prayers in Gethsemane suggest that he knew he was in for a difficult time. Whether he knew he would end up on the cross, or even planned it, though, becomes irrelevant. For his fate was taken out of his hands.

Before his arrest, he could choose how he would teach. He could use words. Or he could use action, like the donkey or the Temple, the washbasin or the bread. But once in the hands of the authorities, he could teach *only* by example.

That example—whether he planned it or not—proved to be the most powerful teaching of his life. For instead of merely taking the side of the poor and the oppressed, he literally became one of them.

Measured only by money, poverty is relative. A single mother on a remote reserve and a single mother in downtown Calgary may receive comparable welfare allowances, but one has much readier access to medical care, education, and vocational guidance than the other. And compared to the poor in Afghanistan, Bolivia, or Ethiopia, both those mothers are unimaginably rich.

But it's not money—nor even the lack of money—that marks poverty. The single factor that identifies the poor, in any nation, anywhere in the world, is lack of choice. They are not in control of their own fate.

Middle-class, relatively affluent, Canadians, can *choose* to live in simpler lifestyles. With noble motives, we can give up fine clothes or fancy cars; we can recycle our garbage; we can flee the urban treadmill and try to live off the land. But we do so by our choice. As long as we have that freedom, we do not belong to the poor.

The real poor, regardless of income or possessions, lack those choices. They can't flee the squalid slums of Calcutta or Capetown; they can't escape the violence of Beirut or Belfast; they can't change the government that grinds them beneath the millstones of economic policy in Mexico or Mozambique. They can't give their children a better chance of survival by providing fresh milk or vaccinations. They don't have such choices. Forces greater than themselves move them about the board of life like pawns.

If the poor, the oppressed, sought only their own survival, they would act like animals, clawing and scratching to further their own fortunes. Sometimes that does happen. But often—as countless missionaries and slum workers and relief agencies will attest—it does not.

Something else often matters even more than their own survival. They want to respect themselves. They don't want to be ashamed of themselves, should they survive.

The cross of Jesus offers them that hope. In his loss of freedom, they recognize their own situation. In his behavior when he could no longer control his own destiny, they see what they could be. That is why the poor and the oppressed all over the world have recognized Jesus as their savior.

Some of the rich and comfortable in the same countries also profess Christian faith. But I suggest that there's an instantly recognizable distinction. The comfortable ones pay attention to what Jesus *said*. The poor pay attention to what he *did*.

And what he did was die a miserable, agonizing, undeserved death.

We should not glorify the cross. Some paintings have portrayed Jesus reigning regally from the cross, gazing serenely down on his gathered subjects, his arms almost extended in blessing. You can still find these "Christus Victor" pictures in religious supply catalogs. Such a portrayal reveals at best a terrible ignorance; at worst, deliberate distortion.

If you want to understand better what the cross must have been like, find yourself any horizontal bar or rail, reasonably high off the ground. Grab the bar, with your hands stretched as far apart as you can reach. Let your weight hang by your arms. See how long you can hang there before the pain becomes excruciating, before your shoulders feel as though they're being pulled from their sockets. How long before you have to let go? Two minutes? Five minutes? Fifteen minutes?

Now imagine hanging there for hours, even days. Imagine having a railway spike hammered through your wrists to support your weight, and another driven through both ankles, pulverizing the bones in its way.

Imagine, too, hanging naked in the desert sun. If you've ever suffered through a serious sunburn, imagine not being able to escape the sun at all. Imagine blistering, even charring, as the inexorable rays sear deeper and deeper into your already scorched skin.

And imagine all this with nothing to drink, your lips cracking, your tongue puffing up, blackening...

By comparison with other victims of crucifixion, Jesus was lucky. He died after only about six hours of this torture (Mark 15:25, 34–37). Others often survived for days, until their bodies could no longer tolerate the dehydration, the sunburn, the pain. Their lungs filled with fluid. They couldn't hold their heads up any more; their heads flopped forward, constricting the windpipe... With a supreme effort, they might manage to lift their heads for one more shuddering gulp of air, before their heads flopped again...

Christians for centuries have studied what are called the "Seven Last Words of Christ" (Matthew 27:46; Mark 15:34; Luke 23:33–46; John 19:25–30). Scholars argue about variations in what each gospel claims Jesus said from the cross. (And whether Jesus really said it, or if later authors added what they thought he *ought* to have said).

But in concentrating on the words, we miss the real point—in six hours, that's *all* he was able to say!

Nothing in the Bible suggests that Jesus was at a loss for words at any time during his preaching ministry. But on the cross, he could gasp out no more than seven short sentences.

Guido Rocha, a Brazilian sculptor, came as close as any artist to capturing the real experience of crucifixion. Rocha portrayed a tortured body of skin-and-bones, emaciated by ill-treatment, teeth knocked out by brutality, hanging on the cross, screaming in agony. Most North Americans turn their heads away from Rocha's version of the crucifixion. They don't want to think about anyone dying that way. But that's how it happened—and still happens.

Rocha recognized the parallel between the torture of Jesus, and the torture of countless victims of repressive regimes around the world. The main difference is that modern torturers use slightly more sophisticated technologies. They apply electric shock—to the ears, the testicles, the vagina... They drown their victims, then resuscitate them, and then drown them again... They inject chemicals that cause raging fever, or depression, or uncontrollable itching...

That's why the victims of the world still identify with Jesus in their own misery. That's why the outcasts, untouchables, refugees, have most readily welcomed the Christian message. In country after country, missionaries have tried to influence the elite, to convert the upper crust, to spread the good news from the top down. And time after time, the elite have rejected Jesus. They don't want the cross. They don't want a symbol that speaks of vulnerability, of helplessness, even of defeat.

But the dregs of society do. They accept Jesus as savior because they can believe that, like him, they are better, they are worth more, than the fate that life has dealt them. They recognize that his fate, like theirs, was undeserved.

The latrine cleaner in India; the Ethiopian mother, trying with dry teats to nurse her dying baby; the Canadian child, born with AIDS, third-hand victim of a self-indulgent father's search for sexual adventures; the grandmother thrown out of work by a distant corporate takeover; the husband, grieving over a wife killed in a freak car accident—none of these ever feel that they have shaped their own fates. All cry out, in one way or another, "Why me, God? Why him? Why her?"

To each, the cross offers the promise that an undeserved fate is not necessary the end of the story.

### Reading: Luke 23:33–46
### The death of Jesus

*Are you old enough to have thought about your own death?*
*How do you expect to die, when the time comes?*
*How do you think the poor, the oppressed,*
*might expect to die?*
*Which death is more like Jesus'?*

**Day 46**  *Saturday*

Our son Stephen had an inquiring, scientific mind.

In his confirmation class, he had a terrible time with Genesis. Especially the first chapter. It didn't correspond to his science studies. "How can I believe that God created the world in six days when I know that it took millions of years?" he would ask.

We argued about that. We enjoyed arguing. We tried to get at different ways of knowing, different perspectives on truth, different levels of scientific sophistication. But somehow we never dealt with the difference between *knowing* and *believing*.

For Stephen, I suspect that the two were the same. You couldn't believe something unless you knew it.

I would probably have put it the other way around. You could believe something, and if you waited, in time you could find the proof you needed to know it.

Both our views missed an essential point.

When Stephen died of cystic fibrosis, I was there. Before we left the hospital, I gave a final hug to his body that was already stiffening and cooling. I *knew*, beyond any question of doubt, that he was dead.

But I didn't *believe* it.

For months, as I drove up our street, I caught myself watching for his long gangling legs striding up the sidewalk, so that I could stop and give him a lift.

When I did something stupid, like letting the bottom fall out of the garbage bag, I found myself listening for his scorn, uttered in that special tone of disgust that sons reserve for fathers.

Camping catalogues arrived, and I instinctively pored over them for equipment we might use on our next hike.

I lived in a kind of limbo, grieving for his loss, yet somehow constantly vigilant for that absent presence.

I knew he was dead. But I didn't live as if he were.

That's the difference between knowing and believing.

Knowing something doesn't necessarily affect the way you live. But believing something does.

**Reading: I John 1:1–4
Testimony of an eye witness**

*You **know** about the Crucifixion and Resurrection.
But do they make any difference
when you're standing in line at the post office?
Or washing the car?
What would help you **believe** them
so that they really make a difference
in your life?*

# Session Six

## Purpose
This is the concluding session. It tries to draw together the theme of teaching through actions that has run through all the sessions, with particular emphasis on the actions of the trial and crucifixion.

Because this is intended to be Lenten study, there is no session dealing with Easter morning. Participants should, however, to continue their own reading and meditation to the Easter reading.

## Preparation
All participants should have read Days 40–46, including Palm Sunday and Good Friday.

Set up chairs and facilities as usual.

Obtain a cross (for A Roman Catholic group) or a crucifix (for a Protestant group).

Have on hand pita bread and grape juice for the concluding agape meal. If several people give leadership, be sure to rehearse first. (And if you follow all the suggestions for that meal, be sure you use an old tablecloth, and have sufficient covering on the carpet!)

## Getting started
Open with prayer and/or singing, as usual.

Welcome any newcomers.

Tell people you want to know their instant reaction when they see something you will show them. For Protestant study groups, show a crucifix, with a figure of Jesus on it; Roman Catholic study groups should use a bare Protestant cross.

## Getting involved
Brainstorm those instant reactions, writing responses onto a flipchart or blackboard. Some comments may produce laughter; others confusion. They all count equally.

Also invite second thoughts. Have people reconsidered their first reactions, or supplemented those first reactions with later thoughts? Especially encourage people to share their feelings when they saw the cross/crucifix. (Protestant reactions to a crucifix, for example, might range from "I'm uncomfortable seeing someone on the cross," to "Do we all have to become Roman Catholics?")

## Starting the thoughts
Draw attention to the range of reactions.

Note that the Crucifixion has always produced diverse reactions. Paul wrote about preaching "Christ crucified, a stumbling block to Jews and foolishness to Gentiles…" (1 Corinthians 1:23).

Draw attention to some of the reasons why the poor and oppressed, all over the world, identify with the Crucifixion (found in Day 45, Good Friday).

Point out how easily Jesus could have avoided being crucified. Jesus apparently knew that Judas intended to betray him(Matthew 26:20–25; Mark 14:17-21; Luke 22:21-23; John 13:21–28). He could have foiled the plot by changing his habits; but he didn't.

Day 40, Palm Sunday, suggests what Jesus might have hoped to show people by his behavior during his trial, and later, his Crucifixion. Read the "untold parable," in the Palm Sunday section, and re-phrase the concluding paragraphs as questions: Where does the parable end? On the cross? Or Easter morning? What difference does it make?

## Grounding thoughts in scripture

Allow a few moments for silent reflection.

Read the whole of Mark's narrative of the arrest, trial, crucifixion, and resurrection—Mark 14:32–16:8. Because it is such a long passage, do not attempt to read it in unison. Rather, choose two or more people who can read this passage with the kind life and vitality they might put into telling a children's story.

## Applying new understandings to life

Divide into smaller groups, as appropriate. Use the following questions to stimulate discussion, or create your own questions based on Days 40–46.

1. *Does it bother you that the message of Christ seems more readily accepted in other countries by the poor, the uneducated, the outcasts than by the leaders and upper classes?* Does the unwillingness of the elite imply failure of our missionaries? Or a repudiation of our own faith? Does association with the dregs of society bother us?

2. *What might have happened to the Christian faith, and the Christian church, if Jesus had been pardoned and set free?*

## Putting it together

If you have divided into several groups for discussion, gather together again.

Invite participants to volunteer insights they may have gained during the discussion.

## Closing

Suggest that the early church remembered Jesus through some of the actions he shared with them.

Read Luke 23:13–34. Emphasize verses 30–31, on their recognizing Jesus in the breaking of bread.

Explain that to concentrate on the actions, rather than on too-familiar words, we shall share a symbolic meal in silence.

Carry the pita bread around so that all can see it. Perhaps hold it so that some can smell its dry, floury scent. Slowly, tear it apart.

Similarly, in silence, take the pitcher of wine or red juice around for people to look into, to smell, to hold. Pour the wine or juice slowly into cups. Use as many cups as you decide you need, whether individual or common cups. (The cups should be big enough to provide more than a symbolic sip.)

*If you have enough nerve*, pour the last of the red wine/juice over the tablecloth, like Moses splashing the blood of the covenant over the altar, likef the shedding of Jesus' blood. (Make sure it's an old cloth, and that you have plastic on the floor to catch drips.)

Remember—all this takes place without words....

Gesture to the people, to come forward, to break off a piece of the bread, to drink from one of the cups. Leaders should mingle with the participants as they come forward, and break bread in their turn.

Have people join hands around the table.

Break the silence to pronounce a commissioning and benediction.

**Day 47**                              *Easter Sunday*

# *Rabboni!*

It's hard to get worked up about Jesus' death when you know it's only until Sunday morning.

Michael Farris, a minister at historic St. Andrew's Presbyterian Church in downtown Toronto, has a gift for putting illuminating ideas into unforgettable phrases. Of the shallowness of our celebration of Easter, he said: "Most Christians treat Easter like a toaster. We drop Jesus into the ground on Good Friday and wait for him to pop up again on Easter morning!"

Knowing the end of the story gives us an unfair advantage over Jesus' followers. We know about Easter. They didn't. When they gathered at the foot of the cross, they knew just one thing—that it was over. All that they had done, had experienced, for three years or so—it was all over.

There was no hope. The cross offered no reprieves, no stays of execution, no last minute phone calls from the governor. Once the victim was fastened to the cross, the only possible outcome was death. And death is forever.

That was the hardest thing for us to face after our son Stephen died. That we would never see him again. Never. Never hear his laugh again, never argue about who got the car, never keep his dinner warm in the oven...

Never.

It's a terrible, aching, empty feeling. And everyone who has lost a child, a partner, a parent, a dear friend, knows it.

That was what the disciples felt, when Jesus was crucified.

Unless we can remember that feeling, we can't begin to understand what Easter felt like. Because we'll still be expecting Jesus to pop up, like toast.

Mary certainly didn't expect to see him, when she came to the tomb early that Easter morning.

It had probably been the worst three or four days of her life. She had come to Jerusalem, along with the other women who had traveled with Jesus and the disciples, looking after them. She had stayed with them in Bethany—she may even have been the woman who anointed Jesus with perfume there. With a woman's intuition, she may have sensed his tension, may have recognized how close the end was coming.

And then, the night of the Last Supper, he didn't come back to Bethany. Late, very late, almost near dawn, some of the disciples would have come racing through the night, hysterical, gasping out the tale of his arrest.

No one would sleep any more that night. They would all hurry back into Jerusalem, perhaps to join John and Peter at the High Priest's house, perhaps to hang around the fringes at Pilate's residence—grabbing for any scrap of information, any scrap of hope.

Was Mary among the crowd who preferred to free a murderer instead of the man who had saved her from her past? When the crowd shouted "Crucify him! Crucify him!" did her voice choke in her throat as she tried desperately to persuade someone, anyone, to take his side?

Certainly, she was at Calvary. With the other women, she stood and watched.

She longed to touch him, to comfort him, to sooth his pain, to hold him in her arms and to comfort him.

But she couldn't.

At first, every thought, every prayer, would have

urged him to keep struggling. "While there's life there's hope," she would tell herself—or some Aramaic equivalent of that saying. And she would cling to that hope. She'd find herself breathing in his rhythm, as if that could give him strength.

But she couldn't.

As she saw how much effort each breath took, her hope would begin to fade. She'd start to realize that her hope was really for herself, because she couldn't imagine her life without him. Slowly, as she sensed his agony, as she heard him suck in each shuddering breath, she began to realize that the only hope for him was death.

And she would begin to say, "Please let him die, Lord. Let him die. But not with this breath. Not quite yet...."

Until even that hope faded.

Her eyes must have been too full of tears to see, but still she could listen. Listen... to each breath, dragged into his lungs by aching muscles straining against the relentless pull on his outstretched arms...

People bustled by, heading into or out of Jerusalem. The soldiers on duty tossed dice, and told dirty jokes, and laughed. A few, prompted by the priests, tossed jeers and taunts at the dying man, and moved on. The other victims screamed out their anger, their pain. But over all the clamor, she could hear, like a knife carving her belly open, the sound of each breath....

And then there were no more.

I know how she felt. For I have been there too.

As they moved his chilling, stiffening body into a tomb, so that he wouldn't get tossed onto the garbage dump like a lump of carrion to be consumed by the vultures and by the fires that smoldered night and day, the sound of those last breaths must still have echoed, somewhere deep inside her empty soul. But by then the Sabbath was starting, the Jewish day of rest. She longed to go to anoint his body, to care for him one last time, even in death...

But she couldn't.

All through that endless Sabbath, she had wept, and waited.

Early the next morning, she came to the tomb, hoping to be able to offer him one last gift of her love, one last act of devotion.

But his body was gone. Whoever had taken it had robbed her of her last chance. She didn't even have his corpse to cry over any more.

Is it any wonder that when she saw someone through her tears, she cried out, frantically: "Tell me where you have taken him...."

Then she heard her name.

"Mary."

She knew the voice. She knew the person. He was not dead. He lived.

In that instant, all the pain, all the loss, lifted off her. The endless waiting, the tears, the agony, the bleakness of the rest of her life—it was all gone.

And all of that relief, that joy, came bursting forth in one word: "Rabboni."

The word goes by so quickly when we read it in the Bible (John 20:11–16). But if we could hear it as she said it, none of us would ever have any doubts about the reality of Easter.

*Another chance...*

## Currents

If you enjoyed reading *Last Chance*, why not enjoy Jim Taylor's writing on a more frequent basis?

Subscribe to **Currents**, Jim Taylor's newsletter. It contains the same kind of informal, personal incidents coupled with religious insight.

**Currents** is published five or six times a year, for an annual subscription of $10 Canadian. (Prices subject to increase; $4 higher outside Canada.)

To subscribe, or to request a free sample copy, write to

**Currents** subscriptions
Wood Lake Books Inc.
Box 700, Winfield, BC, Canada, V0H 2C0

## Wood Lake Books also publishes:

- a best selling lectionary-based Sunday school curriculum, *The Whole People of God.*
- a hymnbook, *Songs for a Gospel People,* produced as a supplement to the hymnbook used by the Anglican and United Churches of Canada.
- a clergy journal, ***pmc:*** *Practice of Ministry in Canada,* for an ecumenical board composed of six denominations.
- a wide selection of books on the Christian faith.

For a free catalog, write to
**Wood Lake Books Inc.**
Box 700, Winfield, BC, Canada, V0H 2C0